"True story—I turned in a book proposal calle[d] [...] manuscript. I read hers cover to cover and em[...] [...] my proposal. Kathy already wrote the book and it's a thousand times be[tter] [than] mine would have been.' Every word of *Raise Your Voice* is profound, courageous, and important. We need this right now, and we need this prophetic teacher to lead us."
Jen Hatmaker, author of *For the Love* and *Of Mess and Moxie*

"*Raise Your Voice* is a powerful call to action. The book is full of moving personal stories, excellent writing, and judiciously scattered solid theology. This delightfully written book summoning us to courageous action to promote racial, gender, and economic justice could not come at a better time. Khang calls us to speak out. And she helps us see how to do it."
Ronald J. Sider, Palmer Seminary at Eastern University

"As a reporter and church leader, Kathy Khang has spent her life lending her voice to other people's stories. This book is essential reading for those who wonder about the spiritual power of saying hard truths out loud."
Kate Bowler, Duke Divinity School, author of *Everything Happens for a Reason*

"In a time of social division growing wider every day, so many of us struggle with how to engage in all that is happening around us. Often it's easier to retreat and ignore the chaos and confusion rather than to try to wrestle with how God might have us respond. Kathy Khang challenges us to see that our trust in God's sovereignty is not independent of our responsibility to act. She guides us through why it is biblical for us to learn to use our voice for good, and imperative to stand against injustice in order that our silence might not become complicit."
Vickie Reddy, executive producer, The Justice Conference

"Leaders, artists, writers, and anyone who feels that God has put something in them (everyone!) will be refreshed, challenged, and spurred on. This book is a compass, instead of a map, that helps you navigate terrain that has no roads. Khang's book provides an essential tool for navigating the tricky pathways of following Jesus in real life—evolving social media, racial land mines, and increasingly polarized communities. *Raise Your Voice* is an honest, funny, and utterly practical book. You will want it on your shelf to refer to over and over again."
Nikki Toyama-Szeto, executive director of Evangelicals for Social Action

"Khang's *Raise Your Voice* is a powerful call to use our voices—whether in print, artistic, or social media form—for God's kingdom and glory. As a powerful advocate of justice, her own story is a testament of overcoming one's imposter syndrome, one's cultural inhibitions, and one's gendered expectations. Put together with scriptural insights and Khang's unique dry humor, this book is a great read. It offers practical, loving, and wise lessons on how each of us can speak out and be heard."
Russell Jeung, author of *At Home in Exile*

"In *Raise Your Voice*, Kathy takes us on a journey of excavation as she digs deeply into Scripture and into her own story to write about the power of finding and using one's voice. Her words walk alongside us, push us, and put us on notice that using our voices for the sake of justice, holiness, and truth telling is important and necessary work. As Kathy raises her own voice, she inspires me to do the same."
Amena Brown, spoken-word poet, author of *How to Fix a Broken Record*

"Kathy has spoken up and spoken out with wisdom at great cost to herself. Learn from her expertise. Since there are lessons we can't learn in theory, I urge you to read this book and learn to use your authentic voice in meaningful, authentic ways."
Sandra Maria Van Opstal, author of *The Next Worship*

"We live in a loud, hyperconnected world where finding and using your voice for good can seem like a daunting, if not impossible, charge. And yet all Christians are called to speak the truth in love. So it's more important than ever to find wise and experienced guides for this new terrain. Kathy Khang is one of those guides, and in *Raise Your Voice* she offers insights that are both philosophical and practical, biblically informed and tested in the lab of real-world experience."
Rachel Held Evans, author of *Searching for Sunday*

"Our voices are paramount to our faith and witness! If you've ever found yourself questioning, doubting, or squelching your voice, this book will intimately speak to you. *Raise Your Voice* illuminates the forces—social, cultural, and familial—that seek to silence us and guides us through the wilderness of finding, claiming, and using our voices to seek the kingdom first and live into our created purpose."
Dominique DuBois Gilliard, author of *Rethinking Incarceration*

"As I read *Raise Your Voice* I remembered the times I needed a book like this! I needed its invitation to discover my voice when I felt invisible and voiceless. I needed its mentoring when I started out in leadership, wondering if I could lead in the way I was wired to, rather than fit uncomfortably into a more culturally acceptable mold. I needed its wisdom to help me discern the cost of having a voice and daring to use it, and then its comfort when using my voice ended in hurt. *Raise Your Voice* is here now, and I still received all the things I'd once longed for and more—challenge and empowerment in equal measure. Kathy Khang has crafted a gift for us—receive every page she offers you!"
Jo Saxton, author of *The Dream of You*, cohost of the Lead Stories Podcast

Kathy Khang

WHY WE STAY
SILENT AND
HOW TO
SPEAK UP

RAISE
YOUR
VOICE

IVP Books

An imprint of InterVarsity Press
Downers Grove, Illinois

InterVarsity Press
P.O. Box 1400, Downers Grove, IL 60515-1426
ivpress.com
email@ivpress.com

InterVarsity Press® is the book-publishing division of InterVarsity Christian Fellowship/USA®, a movement of students and faculty active on campus at hundreds of universities, colleges, and schools of nursing in the United States of America, and a member movement of the International Fellowship of Evangelical Students. For information about local and regional activities, visit intervarsity.org.

All Scripture quotations, unless otherwise indicated, are taken from The Holy Bible, New International Version®, NIV®. Copyright © 1973, 1978, 1984, 2011 by Biblica, Inc.™ Used by permission of Zondervan. All rights reserved worldwide. www.zondervan.com. The "NIV" and "New International Version" are trademarks registered in the United States Patent and Trademark Office by Biblica, Inc.™

While any stories in this book are true, some names and identifying information may have been changed to protect the privacy of individuals.

Cover design: David Fassett
Interior design: Daniel van Loon
Images: paint texture: © eugenesergeev / iStock / Getty Images Plus
      dust explosion: © Bruno Gori / Getty Images

ISBN 978-0-8308-4540-8 (print)
ISBN 978-0-8308-8532-9 (digital)

Printed in the United States of America ♾

Library of Congress Cataloging-in-Publication Data
A catalog record for this book is available from the Library of Congress.

P 25 24 23 22 21 20 19 18 17 16 15 14 13 12 11 10 9 8 7 6 5 4 3 2 1

Y 37 36 35 34 33 32 31 30 29 28 27 26 25 24 23 22 21 20 19 18

For the voices

we have yet to learn and hear from

and for

#flymysweet

#runmyson

#eliasneedsahashtag

CONTENTS

THE RISK OF SILENCE VERSUS
THE RISK OF RAISING YOUR VOICE

have kept a journal since I was in second grade. My father encouraged me to use a notebook and write something about each day. Recently my children discovered some of my childhood journals, and as a family we laughed until we cried. "Today I had hot dogs for lunch. It was a good day." Our stomachs cramped with laughter and levity as we recognized, even in the commentary of my seven-year-old self, a bit of my grown-up dry humor because today is Monday and no one has blocked me from Twitter. It's a good day.

Journaling started out as a way to perfect my penmanship but became a creative outlet as well as an exercise of self-reflection, observations, and storytelling. Journaling gave me a way to express my unfiltered self without self-editing or public critique, which I suspect gave me courage to eventually write more. Childhood journaling gave me a physical practice of owning and acknowledging my observations, emotions, experiences, and thoughts. This morphed into a career as a journalist, blogger, and author of this book—a journey of finding my voice in bits and pieces through the past twenty-plus years of life, parenting, and ministry.

The journey includes that time I joined the high school speech team and heard my voice via video recording for the first time. *Do I really sound like that? Is that what I look like when I talk?* There was the first time I saw an Asian American woman preach. *Can women do that? Can women who kind of look like me do that?* There was the time a college professor didn't hear my question because his answer was, "Where did you learn your English? You speak almost without an accent." I thought silently, *I have a Chicago accent when I get angry and/or animated, but what does it matter?* My response was to ask him, "Where did you learn yours?"

There was the first time I challenged an editor on the use of "pro-life and pro-choice" versus "anti-abortion and pro-abortion." (I can't remember which pairing won, but I can still remember how the pounding of my heart sounded in my head.) Then there was the first time I fought to be the reporter on a story about a black community protesting the hiring practices of a Korean-owned beauty supply store in Milwaukee. I walked my pregnant self over to the editors and told them I would be the only one who could get an interview with the storeowner because I bet there was a language issue at play, and as luck would have it, I was the only reporter in that metro Milwaukee newsroom who spoke broken Korean.

More often than not, raising my voice comes at some cost. Outspoken women are often called aggressive, arrogant, or abrasive. My unscientific polling of outspoken women in my social media bubble showed that most of us have been called a witch (and another word that rhymes with witch). People of color face racial and cultural norms and stereotypes that often reward us for silence. For example, Asian Americans are known as the "model minority"—highlighting a large, multi-cultural, intergenerational group of American-born and immigrants as all being successful. The label is used to create a false narrative and dichotomy between Asian Americans who behave, follow the rules, and therefore succeed compared to "the other" racial minorities. Black and brown parents regularly teach their young children how to behave if and when they interact with law enforcement. Those lessons don't include raising your voice as a means of expressing your humanity. Instead, the lesson is to stay as silent as possible. Women of color sit precariously and boldly in the intersection of race and gender, where raising our voices is a subversive, counter-cultural act that can earn us the labels of defiant or threatening: the angry Latina or black woman, the dragon lady, or even Pocahontas. There is mansplaining and whitesplaining, and women of color can't avoid either. There have been times when I was metaphorically and literally silenced in loud rooms.

Shove all of that into my shadow of self-doubt and wrestling with what ambition looks like until life pushed it out of me as if giving birth, and what do you get? You get this book. In many ways, giving birth to a child was easier than giving birth to my voice. I was able to get pregnant fairly easily the first time. I had great prenatal care, incredible health insurance, and easy access to a hospital. From start to finish, it was nine months. This book has been in the making for ten years.

Finding my voice is ongoing, just like the follow-up to giving birth: parenting. Even now I find myself nudging, pushing, encouraging, and learning from my daughter, in her twenties, to speak and dance her voice. Bethany was seventeen when she told her father and me she wanted to study dance.

"I want to be a dancer. There isn't another subject I want to spend four years exploring. I want to go to college but major in dance," she said, holding back tears. We had no framework with which to answer her announcement. My husband, Peter, and I are Korean American—he's American-born while I'm an immigrant. We believe that education is the road to survival, assimilation, and success. Education, and most certainly college, is not for chasing dreams. Education is practical, as it was for my husband, who is a dentist. On the other hand, I started out as a journalist, went into vocational ministry, and now I'm a writer. So I guess I do have a bit of a framework for pursuing slightly impractical dreams. But a dancer? Journalism majors can work for newspapers or go to law school. What is our daughter going to do with a degree in dance? I thought, *Can you even do that? Is that a real degree?*

Bethany stood near the door to our bedroom. She was waiting for a response while I was trying to figure out what to say. *Do you mean major in dance in addition to another major?* No, I knew that's not what she meant. *How will you get a job that pays enough so that you can pay off your student loans?* No. Peter and

I had told ourselves that our kids' vocational choices shouldn't focus on income earning potential and financial security. *How do we explain this to my immigrant parents?* Oh my goodness. There still is a part of me that wants to please my parents and prove we have done a good job raising our children despite the fact that none of our children speak Korean. *What will other people think? Will they think she isn't serious about her future? Will they think she isn't smart enough to study a "real" subject? Why isn't Peter saying anything?* Oh my goodness. I really do still care about what other people think. I'm still working through how or if my kids' choices and behaviors reflect on me as a parent.

Do you know how risky and full of rejection a career as a dancer can be? What if you get injured? What if you don't get a job? What if all of that starts to make you feel like a failure? How can I let you do this if I can't protect you from getting hurt? But at what point am I projecting my personal fears onto my children, stopping me from blessing them into adulthood? Somewhere in that split-second internal dialogue, I saw my daughter standing in front of her parents and took in her words.

"I want to be a dancer," Bethany said with as much courage and self-awareness she could muster. She had come into our bedroom, into our space, to tell us she had been thinking, dreaming, praying, and worrying about the same things we had been. She had been practicing this declaration, this talk. She had learned something deep and profound about how God had wired her, and she wanted to let us know.

It was our fault, really. When she was in the womb, we learned that reading to a baby in utero could favorably impact brain development, so we read the Psalms to her, poetry and song. We put her in ballet and tap in preschool because in soccer she spent more time playing with a teammate's barrettes than learning to kick the ball. We wanted her to do something physical, and she had not yet developed body image issues and was open to wearing tights and leotards. As Bethany grew, she wanted more dance classes. She made the dance team in middle school and then in high school. She didn't seem to mind the pressure or stress of auditions. She actually seemed to thrive in that space, just like deadlines tend to kick me into a different creative and productive gear. But as her parents, in our minds it was still a hobby, albeit an expensive, time-consuming, physically demanding hobby that could look good on a college application. Dance wasn't supposed to be the focus of her college search. It was supposed to be the extracurricular.

Weeks before Bethany verbally told us she wanted to be a dancer, she had already tried to convey the message, and I think I knew it in my gut. It was when we saw her first piece of choreography. Peter and I were speechless. Stunned. How did a seventeen-year-old child, who was crying over a bad haircut just a few weeks ago, envision and then execute a dance about self-awareness and voice? How did she interpret that piece of music and choose the costuming and color scheme? How did she choose placement and movement of each dancer for each measure of music? I had heard her trying out different choreography—rhythmic thuds and thumps followed by music being replayed. I saw her choreography notebook where she had mapped out formations and written down movement notations. She was writing dance, a language she could speak fluently and translate.

The performance was about a group of young women learning to be themselves as they wrestled with the power of the gaze of others and the reflection they saw in a mirror—a prop that Bethany chose based on shape, size, and color. I also noticed that she didn't choose to be the primary dancer of the piece, as had most of the other student choreographers. When the dancers struck their final pose, all sitting in a line with the last dancer holding up the mirror in the air, I caught myself crying, moved at how the dancers had made me think and feel about self-discovery. Maybe we were just being proud parents. But audience members came up to her and to us after the performance (we were easy to spot because she was one of maybe two dancers of color) to congratulate her. One compliment stuck in my heart like a dagger: "That was the most mature and moving piece I've seen in our years of seeing student work." She was just starting.

"I want to be a dancer," Bethany said.

My husband and I realized that we were exactly "those" parents who harbored secret ambitions and plans for their children. We had to come face-to-face with a child, actually now a young woman, who had a deeper sense of who she was than we were willing to acknowledge or see. Would we try to get in God's way, or would we help and free her to develop her talents and her own voice? Would we stay silent, or would we give her our blessing?

My parents blessed me to pursue an undergraduate degree in journalism, but it came with a single string attached. Well into my thirties, my parents didn't hold back the fact they had always hoped allowing me the freedom to major in journalism would mean I would eventually come around and pursue an advanced degree, preferably in law. When I left journalism to go into vocational ministry, they made it clear they thought it was a phase. I knew their not-so-secret hopes came with the best of intentions full of love and faith that I had what it took. Yet every time they said, "It's not too late to go back to law school!" I felt like a failure and had another reason to go back to therapy. I'm sure I have given my daughter and her two brothers plenty of other reasons to seek therapy, but when Bethany said she wanted to be a dancer, I begged God to teach me to be the parent who dreams with her children rather than dictating in not-so-subtle ways what approved paths to success look like.

So I go to therapy off and on, and I write. I learned to write about other people's stories as a reporter, and I learned that reporting just the facts still meant those facts were being filtered, prioritized, and shaped by my writing and my editor's editing. I learned that my writing could be helped by a strong accompanying photograph that captured a moment that couldn't easily be translated into written words. My childhood practice of journaling followed me into adulthood and grew and shifted when I was pregnant with Bethany. I started a separate journal when she was born and then started a new one for each of my pregnancies. Each child has her or his own journal where I've documented the mundane and fabulous. I give voice to my fears, doubts, joys, successes, and failures as a mother. I write down the funny and poignant things each child says—stories they may not remember but are important to know.

That is why I love this book's title, even as I wrestle with the power and danger of a declarative, demanding statement such as "raise your voice." As a parent, I hope to raise my children to grow into adulthood with a sense of their own unique voice. *Raise Your Voice* isn't explicitly about parenting, but it's about the growth and development I'm in part responsible for in my children while I also remain in that process myself. I look at my children and think, *Raise your voice!* while they look to me to set the example. Blessing Bethany to pursue a dance degree was telling her to raise her voice while still figuring out how to bless her, encourage her with our words, support her with our presence at her performances, learn about the industry, send her care packages and letters, provide financial support, and meet her fellow dance majors and faculty.

Without a doubt, being a mom has been part of the journey of finding, losing, and finding again my own voice. In the early days of motherhood I felt like I had lost myself in a sea of sleep deprivation, diapers, sippy cups, playdates, and art projects. Yet God had not forsaken me in a sea of hormones and bodily fluids. Every time I prayed for my children, God was inviting me to raise my voice. Every time I learned what it meant to be a mama bear, I also learned how to raise my voice. Every time I tried to get my kids to help write a thank-you note, I was raising my voice and my child's voice. I learned how I could harm or heal with my voice, literally and figuratively. I learned how to advocate for and be an ally by being a parent.

In the midst of being a mom of young children, I was also figuring out how to be an actual journalist while being the only Asian American and one of the very few people of color while working in three different editorial newsrooms. Raising my voice too much or too often felt like risking job security, especially when I was the only pregnant and then lactating Asian American woman in what were very white, male newsrooms. Sometimes we stay silent because it's easier, because speaking up means taking a risk we don't feel prepared to take or have the energy or support to take. Whether it was the isolation of being the only woman of color at the hospital playgroup or the added level of stress and energy it took to navigate a white, male workplace, I didn't think I had a voice, let alone the time to raise that voice. Sometimes we stay silent because we think that it's our only choice to survive.

I wrote *Raise Your Voice* because I learned that even when I chose to be silent and do nothing, I was still choosing to communicate something. It's a declaration, a request, a warning, and an invitation because I'm convinced too many of us feel like we don't have a voice. You might feel like you're too young or too old. You might be a woman. You might be a person of color. You might identify as LGBTQIA (lesbian, gay, bisexual, transgender, queer, intersex, asexual). You might have a disability or chronic illness. You might be an immigrant or undocumented. You might feel like your experience isn't universal enough to be important or even acceptable. I want you to know that *you have a voice*. God wants you to use it, and the world needs to hear, see, and experience it.

Encouraging Bethany and our sons, Corban and Elias, to raise their voices also meant modeling that for them in ways not defined by my role as their mother and cheerleader but as a neighbor, community member, and writer. Bethany, who just moved into her first apartment post-graduation, is at the beginning of testing out her adult voice, while I'm squarely in mid-journey. As she develops and uses her voice, I learn from her and vice versa. I still keep a journal where I track the books I've read along with all the self-reflection a cup of coffee can fuel, and I still keep my "Bethany" journal of twenty-two-plus years. I'm still learning the importance of finding one's personal voice and stewarding it well in community and for the good of community in a connected world. Even writing this book has been part of a ten-year process of figuring out if I had anything worth writing about and if I could handle whatever friends, critics, and my internal critic might say.

Learning to use your voice is about understanding how we each are created in God's image. It's about the space in which gender, faith, ethnicity, and race converge, adding to the power and beauty of individual voices effectively impacting and shaping the church and the world. It's about knowing deeply how God sees you, grounded in the truth that we are all created in God's image, and using your voice in word, deed, and art to communicate the good news in a messed-up world.

Part 1

WHY
WE STAY
SILENT

Chapter 1

SEEN BUT NOT HEARD

Children should be seen and not heard.

ENGLISH PROVERB

The nail that sticks out gets hammered down.

JAPANESE PROVERB

Even fools are thought wise if they keep silent,
and discerning if they hold their tongues.

PROVERBS 17:28

When I walked into the ballroom, the main session of the conference was already well underway. I was a bit frazzled from my five-hour drive but not too discombobulated to realize immediately that something was wrong. I sat next to a colleague, made eye contact with her, and smiled. Then, uncharacteristically for our relationship, we instinctively reached out for each other's hands. We sat for a few moments holding hands when suddenly I had the urge to cry and found myself holding back emotions and tears I didn't understand. My colleague squeezed my hand to let me know that she knew I was distressed, but I still didn't know why I was feeling what I was experiencing.

After the session ended, my colleague asked me if I was okay and if I had had time to process what had happened at the earlier sessions. I had absolutely no idea what was going on and asked her to explain. There had been a leadership crisis developing behind the scenes between several beloved, respected senior leaders. The relational conflict included racial, gender, and cultural dynamics. My colleague assumed I had seen all of this unfold when she noticed I was getting emotional. We both realized that my emotions and spirit were registering something I hadn't experienced firsthand. She and I both sensed God was giving me a starting point to wrestle with difficult emotions and build up courage. Honestly, it felt weird. I tucked that intense moment into my mental filing system.

On the last night of the conference, our team crowded into a meeting room meant for a group half our size. It was late in the evening, but it was our only chance to hear from a senior leader who knew what had happened and what was still happening. We all listened while carefully shooting nervous glances across the room. I found myself wringing my hands, questions welling up in my mind about what had transpired and why.

When the floor was finally opened for questions, a few people made polite statements thanking the senior leader for coming and filling us in. I kept waiting for someone to ask the questions I was sure more than half of us were wondering: Why had we not met earlier in the week, been updated, and given a chance to respond? Why were we left in the dark until the night before we all were leaving, if not to keep us silent?

I felt my emotions and tears from the beginning of the conference well up. Seriously? No one was going to ask? Fine.

I waited for what I thought was an appropriate time, raised my hand, waited to be acknowledged, took a deep breath to keep my tears at bay, and steadied my voice. I don't remember the exact wording of my multipart question, but it didn't matter. Before I could finish, out of the corner of my eye I saw something move across my face. The person sitting next to me, a friend, was listening to my question and heard the direction it was going—and then physically covered my mouth with her hand.

I had been silenced. Literally, physically stopped from speaking up.

I felt embarrassed and deeply ashamed. I was angry and confused, violated and sick to my stomach. I didn't understand how powerful my words and my voice could be until someone made sure I wouldn't be heard.

IF YOU SPEAK, WILL ANYONE HEAR YOU?

The world is a noisy place. Smart phones. Smart watches. Alerts. Notifications. Social media. Satellite radio. Streaming video. News 24/7. On any given Sunday morning in church, don't be surprised if you hear a guitar or keyboard playing softly in the background during the announcements or prayer. Culturally, it's almost as if we are uncomfortable with silence.

Yet when people rise up and collectively make some noise, public displays of personal opinions are often closely monitored and critiqued. I was raised to believe public protests were dangerous, disrespectful, disruptive, and, therefore, inappropriate.

Those adjectives have been used frequently to describe recent protests against white supremacy and for immigration reform.

I first learned that public protests were considered inappropriate after finding myself accidentally attending and then willingly participating in protests against increasing US military presence in South Korea while on a trip there, my homeland. I had left South Korea as an eight-month-old and returned as a college student on a church missions/cultural enrichment trip. I developed friendships with Korean college students who were active in the student protest movements. They spoke about feeling voiceless but also about finding power and common purpose as they protested together and leaned on one another for courage. I learned about liberation theology and *minjung* theology, an indigenous theology born out of Korea's post-war struggle and emergence. I honestly didn't know what to do with it all, especially the theology that tapped into a cultural value of community and harmony that didn't exist in the individualistic theology of the West. At first I listened to the history of the student protest movements, safely observing from the sidelines. But within the first month of our trip, most of our group was participating—we learned the chants, carried bandanas to protect ourselves from the tear gas, and were well-versed in making Molotov cocktails.

It turns out that government monitoring of public protests doesn't happen just in the United States. My uncle, who worked for the South Korean government, showed up completely unannounced one random afternoon at the office where we were meeting. He came carrying pizzas, but his presence was an indirect warning to make sure his niece stayed out of trouble, stayed safe, and stayed silent. I wouldn't take part in a public protest for another twenty years.

I tell that story because I still feel new to exercising my right to peaceably assemble. It's not something I have always been drawn to. Using my voice has mostly been through speaking and writing, not using my body in protest. But as my convictions have deepened and life experiences have changed me, I've chosen to march in support of #BlackLivesMatter and against the Dakota Access Pipeline, the Muslim travel ban, and a recent president. Bethany and I also marched together with three Asian American friends at the Women's March on Washington in January 2017 because we wanted to make sure our voices were both seen and heard as Christian women of color. I find the news coverage, police presence, and public commentary around those events fascinating. Different voices—such as women, people of color, LGBTQIA—are critiqued, praised, dismissed, ignored, or judged on who should or should not participate. Why can't someone participate if they want to?

Public protest and free speech are protected under the law, but that doesn't mean there aren't consequences. There are days when it feels like you can't win. If you stay silent, you might find yourself on the wrong side of history. Or you might be seen and heard, and then wish you hadn't. Demonstrations from Charlottesville to Venezuela have proved deadly and dangerous for protesters. You might find yourself completely misunderstood after speaking up. Even worse, instead of believing your accounts of experiences with racism or injustice, people may question your perspective or accuse you of exaggerating, lying, or playing the race card. They reframe your story and change it to make it appear that you were actually the aggressor. After being attacked for sharing, you might even begin to question your memory of the experience. But then you'll realize the truth—you *were* the victim of a racist or unjust incident and now have been gaslighted by those who don't want to believe you.

It's no wonder people are opting out of social media, trading in their smartphones, and deciding it's better to stay out of the public and even private square. It's become a common Lenten practice for some to give up social media or temporarily deactivate their social media accounts. I have one friend who has gone back to using a basic flip phone to keep him from engaging in the public sphere when he's away from a computer.

At some point in our lives, we learn to communicate, whether verbally or non-verbally. But most of us are also taught to silence ourselves or to stay out of the conversation for self-preservation. We are taught to avoid conflict, keep the peace, and keep our personal opinions to ourselves because we're told that speaking out doesn't actually affect change. However, self-preservation takes on a different sense of urgency and meaning as the national and global political landscape continues to shift. The North American church is again engaging in conversations around race and justice, but because of its past failures and current blind spots, the conversation often resorts to simplified binaries such as white and black, men and women, privileged and lack of privilege, citizen and undocumented—and the refusal to dig deeper into racist and unjust systems can widen the chasm.

I believe that Christians desire and can handle more complexity. Race and reconciliation can no longer be framed solely as a justice issue but rather as core to the gospel, theologically grounded in the *imago Dei* (the image of God). As Christians, if we truly believe we are all created in God's image, and that God the Creator had a hand in developing, creating, and shaping not just our embodied souls but also the places and spaces we steward and have dominion over, then reconciliation with one another is not merely an option—it's part of God's mandate. It requires us to speak up and speak out.

In order to do so, we need to address personal development, which happens within the context of community. In some communities, certain voices are erased and suppressed while others are amplified and elevated. The concept of "voice" isn't only what is said or written but also includes how identity is expressed in words and deed. Voice is not limited to what comes out of my mouth but out of my being.

The Latin word vox, meaning "voice," and the related word *vocāre*, meaning "to call," give us the root **voc** or **vok**. Words from the Latin *vox* or *vocāre* have something to do with the voice or with calling. Anything **voc**al is produced by the voice. A **voc**ation is the work that someone is called to do as a job. To e**vok**e is to call forth. To in**vok**e is to call on for aid or protection. To pro**vok**e is to call forth another's anger. The word **voice** also has *vox* as its root.[1]

The challenge to raise your voice is about doing the good work of the good news. It's about calling forth others: an invocation for all and a provocation to some. Our lives should affect the world around us if we are bearers of God's image as well as an embodiment of good news. Living as a Korean American Christian woman, there is something critical about speaking from a place of wholeness and uniqueness that makes my voice part of a community but also uniquely mine. It fills in the blanks left in others' stories. When more of us from different intersections and margins raise our voices, we live a fuller picture of the good news.

THE STORIES WE TELL

I had the honor of watching my friend, author and artist Amena Brown, raise her voice at Soul City Church in Chicago. Amena told us a story about her grandmother and the care she put into packing food for family members who were traveling. Her grandmother would carefully wrap a slice of cake in waxed paper and put fried chicken in a paper towel and foil. These lovingly packed meals were important to African Americans in the time before the passage of the Civil Rights Act, when black travelers didn't know if they would be able to find a restaurant that would serve them.

As I recall Amena's performance, mannerisms, and imitation of her grandmother's speech and cadence, I can see how the warm memories of food dovetailed into a story of racial injustice. Amena can tell this story because of who she is and who her people are. And while I can share her story here, I can't possibly embody the story because it's not in my bones or blood.

But I can share the story of how my grandmother, who was a child in Korea during Japanese rule, was widowed before she turned forty while raising five children and how she never remarried. I can tell you how she refused to tell me her Japanese name, but did tell me about why she choose not to remarry—because she would have been forced to prioritize her role as wife over her role as mother, even though it was difficult to live as a single mother in her patriarchal culture.

Amena's grandmother and my grandmother. Two different women, two different periods in history—but injustice didn't silence them or stop them from acting on their own behalf and on behalf of their families. We need to give voice to these uniquely embodied stories. We need their complexity and beauty. And this is where I see my story, and the various stories of diverse communities, and the biblical stories of Esther, the bleeding woman, Moses, the women at the cross, and the resurrection colliding—in identity formation, in community, and in advocacy against racism and misogyny.

Most of the books I've read and speakers I've heard on the topic of voice and identity have been white men or women with little nuance and contextualization for individuals and communities that reside both on the margins and simultaneously in the intersections. I believe we need to address voice and identity through the intersections of race, ethnicity, gender, and class, as well as in personal and public spheres of communication. The growing focus on racial reconciliation and the pursuit of justice only highlights the lack of nonwhite and nonblack voices, especially but not exclusively in evangelical circles. Women of color need to be part of the reconciling work of the gospel. We all need to understand that voice, identity, and agency are given by God but often underdeveloped or ignored in people on the margins. We need to be seen and heard.

ETHNICITY AND PLACE IN OUR STORIES

People on the margins and in the intersections need to see themselves and their stories in the conversation, but they also need to learn to tell those stories. A common retelling of the book of Esther is through a white male lens: Esther is the winner of a beauty pageant, and the titles of king and queen are filtered through a western understanding of power and some degree of equality if not equity and agency for both king and queen. But when I look at Esther's story I see racial passing and the implications of a young, disenfranchised woman who has assimilated but not completely lost her culture accepting the opportunity to seek justice for her people in a misogynistic culture. I see how Esther couldn't have come to her journey if it were not for the prior example of Queen Vashti choosing first to speak out by refusing the king's demands for what amounts to a lap dance for his friends.

Esther was both Esther and Hadassah. She was a Jewish woman living crossculturally in exile in Persia. Her social location and ability to navigate her identity impacted how she was seen and heard, and how she saw herself and eventually used her voice.

Like Esther, I grew up knowing about my ethnicity and place. I was a Korean who immigrated to the United States. I became Korean American and then later Asian American. I wasn't just one or the other. I was both, and it can still be confusing. Americans are stereotypically loud where Asians are stereotypically quieter. America is a young country perhaps just on the front end of puberty whereas Korea's existence goes back centuries.

Somewhere between being Korean and American is where I learned I was supposed to raise my hand and speak up in school, but if I raised my hand too often classmates would say I was trying too hard or showing off. I also learned that if I told teachers about the racial bullying I experienced, the perpetrators retaliated with even more ignorance and force. At home and at my Korean immigrant evangelical church, I was supposed to listen and stay quiet. Pastors and spiritual leaders spoke with authority, and they were all men. I was supposed to listen to my elders and defer to their judgment. Each space had a different set of rules.

In college the conflicting messages took root internally and marked the beginning of my journey with imposter syndrome: the internal voice that tells you that you aren't qualified to do, say, or be whatever it is that you are actually doing, saying, or being. It tells you that you have been hired not because you were the best candidate but because a quota had to be met. It tells you that at any moment you will be found out for being less qualified, incompetent, and an imposter or fraud. American psychologists Pauline Clance and Suzanne Imes coined the phrase, describing it as a feeling of "phoniness in people who believe they are not intelligent, capable or creative despite evidence of high achievement." These people (also known as me and some of you) want to achieve but also "live in fear of being 'found out' or exposed as frauds."[2] There is some research indicating a possible correlation between imposter syndrome and introversion as well as people who experience anxiety in multiple situations because imposter syndrome itself is an anxiety-driven experience.[3]

BEING FOUND OUT

Imposter syndrome isn't unique to women, and while it was given a name in the twentieth century, feeling like a fraud is not a modern conundrum. One of the first recorded examples of this internalized self-doubt is in the biblical story of Moses. Hebrew baby boys were supposed to be killed by order of the Pharaoh, but Hebrew midwives "feared God and did not do what the king of Egypt had told them to do; they let the boys live" (Exodus 1:17). Moses was one of those surviving babies; he was adopted by Pharaoh's daughter and grew up in Pharaoh's family.

As an adult, Moses comes to understand that he is Jewish: "One day, after Moses had grown up, he went out to where his *own* people were and watched them at their hard labor. He saw an Egyptian beating a Hebrew, one of his *own* people" (Exodus 2:11, emphasis added).

What we learn in the rest of the chapter is that Moses' understanding of his identity and his internal bent toward justice is where his struggle with imposter syndrome pivots. He wrestles with his identity (is he Egyptian or Hebrew?). He comes to understand his motivation (a sense of justice and freedom that ought to be afforded to all people). And he tests out his voice. Only then does he begin to become who he was meant to be.

Moses, who knows he is Hebrew, sees an Egyptian beating a Hebrew. Later, believing that no one is watching, he kills that Egyptian in an attempt to serve justice. Before we get all high and mighty about Moses being a murderer and wrap it up neatly by saying God uses the most unlikely people, we need to acknowledge that Moses had lived a life of privilege while watching his own people suffer. What does watching your own people suffer do to a person? Moses isn't just an unlikely leader because he is also a murderer. He is an unlikely leader because he has yet to come to an understanding of his identity.

The next day, perhaps emboldened by his secret act of revenge, Moses tries to intervene in a fight between two Hebrew workers. The problem? The two Hebrew workers don't see Moses as one of their own. "The man said, 'Who made you ruler and judge over us? Are you thinking of killing me as you killed the Egyptian?' Then Moses was afraid and thought, 'What I did must have become known'" (Exodus 2:14).

The question of identity doesn't end there. Pharaoh hears what happened and tries to kill Moses, the young man who was raised by his daughter. Moses runs, hides, and makes a life for himself among another tribe. He voices his loss of home and identity when he names his son Gershom: "I have become a foreigner in a foreign land" (Exodus 2:22). Talk about passing your issues on to your children.

For the next two chapters of Exodus, we witness Moses working through his imposter syndrome, culminating in communicating with God through a burning bush. What I wouldn't do for an actual burning bush to make it clear to

me that God is the one calling me to do something! Lucky
Moses gets a real burning bush. However, at some point we
all encounter a metaphoric burning bush and experience God:
a fire that burns but doesn't consume, a source of energy that
doesn't flame out or destroy the host.

What is Moses' response to hearing God call him by name
from the flames?

"Here I am" (Exodus 3:4).

I'm not certain I would know what to do if I audibly heard
my name being called out from a fire, but I'm fairly certain
I wouldn't use Moses' words. It's important to consider that
Moses is willing to be fully present and that he allows his
curiosity to take over any sense of confusion or fear. Moses
is in the wilderness leading a flock of livestock. He has
responsibilities that people depend on him to complete. We
don't know what happens to his flock, but we do know what
Moses does: he stops what he's doing and pays attention
to God.

God commands Moses to take off his sandals. As a Korean
American, I know that you don't track outside dirt inside a
home, so this command would make sense to me if Moses
were entering a house. But in this context, Moses' sandals
were a symbol of his privilege as a free person[4] who had some
status or degree of wealth.[5] An encounter with God not only
renders the space holy but also renders a symbol of privilege
absolutely unnecessary.

Like Moses, in order for us to begin the journey of finding
and using our voices, we need to be fully present and also
recognize and take off whatever privilege as best we can. Using

your voice is holy work, and God doesn't need or require you to have an advanced degree or wealth. God certainly can leverage that privilege and challenge us to think of privilege differently, but the privilege itself is not necessary. And for a woman, an immigrant, and perpetual foreigner in this land, that is good news.

Fortunately for us, Moses' experience with imposter syndrome doesn't end neatly because reality is rarely neat. Moses and God have a conversation, almost a call and response, as God invites Moses to be the one to bring the Israelites out of captivity. Moses responds by asking, "Who am I that I should go to Pharaoh and bring the Israelites out of Egypt?" (Exodus 3:11).

Just moments before this, Moses was present and ready, but now he has a quick change of heart. I'm sure that Moses isn't the only person who has instantly experienced this type of buyer's remorse.

But Moses isn't chickening out. He's doing exactly what any one of us might do when presented with an opportunity to take a risk, to do something a little outside of our comfort zone, to be a leader when we think of ourselves as followers, or to say something that might be controversial or political. When we find ourselves questioning ourselves, doubting and hesitating, we can try to find affirmation and a deeper understanding of ourselves by inviting others to give us feedback or pray with us. We can meet with a spiritual director or a life coach. We can be open to the wisdom and input of wise friends. Ultimately, we will find ourselves asking God about our identity.

God's answer to Moses doesn't satisfy my personal longing for words of affirmation and praise for a job well done. God's answer is simple: "I will be with you" (Exodus 3:12). That's it. God is with Moses. God is with us. Our identity is known and defined by the very One who created the universe in all its diversity; it's complex and at the same time beautifully simple. God is able to identify us not by the lowest common denominator—we are all human—but by knowing precisely how Moses' story is unique and yet intersects with ours in present day.

I'd like to think that knowing that God knows me better than any game of identity politics I can play is enough to give me the confidence to do some crazy things, but it isn't and it wasn't for Moses. Thank goodness for reality.

Moses isn't satisfied with God's answer and has more questions: "Suppose I go to the Israelites and say to them, 'The God of your fathers has sent me to you,' and they ask me, 'What is his name?' Then what shall I tell them?" (Exodus 3:13).

Moses is asking God about theology and knowledge. This makes sense when you consider that Moses probably received some formal education in the Pharaoh's palace, but at this point he is a shepherd. Moses asks God how to explain God to the Israelites. Viewed in the light of the modern American church, which may be too dependent on advanced degrees, knowledge, theologies, and structures, Moses doesn't have the credentials to be a church leader. With his felony record, I'm not sure if he even could get a job.

The question about theology and knowledge is quickly followed up by Moses' final question: "What if they do not believe me or listen to me and say, 'The LORD did not appear to you'?" (Exodus 4:1).

Friends, this is imposter syndrome turned up to eleven. At this point, God has given Moses a script of how things are going to go down. But Moses doesn't believe he is the right person for the job, even though God appeared to him in a burning bush, called him by name, patiently answered his questions, and gave him instructions. But Moses still isn't sure. I'm totally with Moses—I get him.

STRUGGLING WITH CREDIBILITY

I'm a Korean American married mother of three with no advanced degree living in the suburbs in the middle of a midlife crisis, wondering how or if my twenty years of vocational ministry can transfer into a different vocation. I write infrequently. I speak even more infrequently. I have been told that I'm a prophetic voice, but I cringe at that description because biblical prophets are lonely and cranky, and I want to be perceived as fun and warm. Oh, and did I mention that I'm a woman of color in ministry?

Almost ten years ago, I supervised a ministry staff team that worked with four distinct student populations with a reach of about three hundred active students. I learned that a group of local Asian American pastors were meeting periodically to talk about ministry and leadership and pray for one another—but I never received an invitation to those meetings.

A few years later, I hired a graduating student leader, a young Korean American man, to join my staff. He fairly quickly received an invitation to attend the pastors' gathering. Holding back tears, I told him that I had never been invited to attend those meetings. Still, with a mix of frustration based on my experience and hope for what he might experience, I told him that I wanted him to go, learn, and speak into that group.

It took him a moment to realize what the significance of the invitation was for him and what the lack of an invitation meant for me. Ten years of ministry wasn't enough credibility to overcome the fact that I am a woman.

Moses struggled with credibility as well. It's almost comical to read God's assurances in Exodus 4 when you realize that Moses is just as insecure as the rest of us. God goes to great lengths to build up Moses: he gives superpowers to Moses' staff, he shows Moses a cool cloak trick involving leprosy, and teaches Moses how to turn water from the Nile into blood. Yet Moses says, "Pardon your servant, Lord. I have never been eloquent, neither in the past nor since you have spoken to your servant. I am slow of speech and tongue" (Exodus 4:10). And if that wasn't enough, Moses then says, "Pardon your servant, Lord. Please send someone else" (Exodus 4:13). This is when I want to laugh at Moses. Who does he think he is?

Oh, wait. Kathy, meet Moses.

Before taking the ministry staff job, I was struggling with what I still struggle with—managing work and family. I was a mom to one preschooler and two grade school children. My internal script screamed, *Who do you think you are trying to lead and grow ministry and develop a staff team while raising three children and being a good wife? I have kids who get sick and want me at their Valentine's Day parties. Please send someone else.*

I suppose if I had kept that thought to myself, it might have been a little different, but instead of talking to God or a burning bush or my backyard fire pit, I shared this internal script with my staff team. I tried to paint a picture of how and where I thought ministry could grow on campus while also externally processing my personal insecurities. I would remind the team, "I am just part-time, so I can't fulfill all of my job responsibilities; also, I have to leave to pick up my sick kid, so I've asked my predecessor to lead the rest of the meeting." Yes, I actually said those things out loud, which doesn't set up expectations well for anyone. My years managing the team weren't my best as a leader, but I learned a lot about imposter syndrome. It can kick your ego and paralyze you.

God knows that Moses has impostor syndrome but essentially gives him no room to back out. God enlists the help of Moses' brother Aaron as a wingman, reminds Moses that his shepherd's staff has superpowers, and pushes Moses out of the wilderness. The rest of Exodus reminds us that just like Moses, whether or not we carry a shepherd's staff, we don't know the power of using our voices until we try it.

CALLED OUT BY GOD

As I sat there in the conference leadership meeting that last night, my mouth was covered but I knew the questions had to be asked. I felt the heat of shame in my cheeks and could feel my heart pounding in my head. I moved my friend's hand off of my mouth, took a deep breath, and continued to speak.

We are silenced by someone else or sometimes by ourselves. Women of color who speak up tend to face swift backlash with labels of being an angry (fill in race or ethnicity) woman. Words are powerful and can be used to free people from captivity or to sentence people into captivity. God created humans to communicate with one another, not so that we would use words and actions to hurt and destroy one another but to be a blessing to one another. God used words to assure Moses of his identity as one beloved and known by the Creator, and then asks Moses to go out and speak up on behalf of the Israelites.

Likewise, we are seen by God and called out of our imposter syndrome wilderness to proclaim freedom and good news to the world. God asks you to raise your voice.

Chapter 2

WHO AM I?

HOW *IMAGO DEI* GIVES US AGENCY AND A VOICE

*C*reation was not meant to be silent. All of creation communicates. Living in the Midwest affords me the privilege of seeing nature announce the start of various seasons. Crocuses and daffodils pushing through the frozen ground and garbage previously hidden under stubborn piles of dirty ice are usually the first signs of spring. Sneezing and red, itchy eyes follow. In the summer, dandelions compete with cicadas, lightning bugs, and mosquitoes. Leaves turn yellow, orange, and red in the crisp fall air. And winter shows up with sleet, snow, ice, and even some sunny January days teasing us that spring isn't far away. Plants communicate by blooming or browning. Fruits and vegetables change size and shape so we know when they are ready for harvest.

I know animals communicate with one another—not just because of animated movies, but because all my neighborhood rabbits tell each other when the strawberries and lettuce are ripe (unless the coyotes have already communicated about the location of said rabbits). But it's also been scientifically proved that animals communicate. Whales use echolocation. Dolphins communicate with one another through a series of clicks, and each has its own unique signature whistle or sound. Birds sing. Dogs bark, wag their tails, or bare their teeth to signal each other or their human friends. Some species can change the appearance of their skin.

Nature communicates with itself. During the August 2017 solar eclipse in the United States, news teams across the path of totality recorded the incredible scene of darkness that descended during the middle of the day, signaling the crickets to start chirping. As the sun came out of hiding, birds started singing as if to announce the sunrise again.

God the Creator built humans with the ability to communicate, connect, and create in order to steward the whole of creation. From the moment a baby is born, we wait for the first cry and then the first real smile. New parents imagine what it will be like to hear a child's first words as well as what that child will grow up to do or become. Our voices are not just the product of our vocal chords. Our voice—our influence and interaction with people and the world around us—is embodied through our words and actions. When we understand our voice, we echo God's character and good news. It's never *only* what we say *or* do. It's not either-or. Our voice is both word and deed.

In Hebrew, the noun *devar* means word and instruction, what is spoken and what action to take. The name of the book of Deuteronomy in Hebrew is *devarim*, the plural form of *devar*. So the book that lays the foundation for the people of Israel in "laws" or "commandments" is named for its words and actions. Deuteronomy 1:1 says, "These are the words Moses spoke to all Israel in the wilderness east of the Jordan" and can be translated as "these are the words that spoke Moses"—a wooden and awkward translation, yet it captures the nuance of the book. These are the words that will shape how Moses and the Israelites will live and be, and he speaks them to the people. Speech, or more accurately speaking, prompts action. Voice is activism.

GOD SPEAKS CREATION

And so we go back to the beginning to understand voice. The biblical and theological foundation through the Genesis account of creation, fall, redemption, restoration, and reconciliation teaches us that our ability to influence—our voice—is never for individual gain and safety but is intended to steward creation and encourage the flourishing of one another in community and in relationship with God.

In Genesis 1 God speaks creation into being, forms human beings in his own image (*imago Dei*), and blesses them. God's image is of three distinct beings, expressions of the Trinity always in relationship with and to one another. The Godhead is never separate from Spirit and Son, yet each has a distinct role—spiritual father/mother, counselor, and physical embodiment. Because God creates humans in his image, it means that we take on characteristics and traits of the triune God, for example as healer or creator, and that we are part of a whole even in our individuality. The blessing we receive from God is "Be fruitful and increase in number; fill the earth and subdue it" (Genesis 1:28). Our role is to steward and care for all of creation. We are to use our voices to create and be creative just like God modeled in his initial act of creation. Our words and deeds are meant to help fill the earth and subdue it. But by the time of the Tower of Babel, it's clear that mankind has misused their words and deeds. They build "a tower that reaches to the heavens, so that we may make a name for ourselves; otherwise we will be scattered over the face of the whole earth" (Genesis 11:4). They wanted to use their voice, influence, and activism to build a city and tower for personal gain and glory.

I sometimes imagine that God watched this and let it go on for a little while before finally deciding to give everyone a break. God doesn't curse the people but instead gives different languages to different people so that they can actually fulfill the creation mandate. This isn't punishment. It also serves as a foreshadowing of Pentecost, where the Holy Spirit gives people the ability to speak in languages they didn't previously know so that they can share the gospel with others.

With Pentecost, God shows that he understands that we need to hear the good news in ways we can understand, including in a language we can understand. Some of us have a primary language but also grew up speaking another language—a mother tongue or heart language. God provides countless languages—heart languages—for people to speak and hear. God also gave us other ways to understand and communicate—for example, through our senses and through the arts. The more you understand who you are, uniquely and individually created, the more you will understand your voice.

VOICE IS IDENTITY, NOT A BRAND

Despite what social media gurus will tell you, your voice is not part of your personal branding or there to expand your platform. You are not a brand. You and I are created in God's image, the *imago Dei*, which means that we can reflect and communicate God's healing and beauty into hopeless, broken, hurt, and empty spaces. Our voice is meant to be and bring good news.

And because we are uniquely created, our voices are also different. We take on the influences and nuances of our social location, gender, race, ethnicity, and sexual identity. It's not only that my voice literally sounds different than my husband's— there are many differences and similarities between us that create our unique voices. Peter is male and I'm female. We are both ethnically Korean and we both experience racism. He has never experienced sexism. He has birthright citizenship in the United States and I'm a naturalized citizen. Peter's father immigrated to the United States after the Korean War to complete his undergraduate studies in Michigan. My parents and I immigrated almost ten years later; my father had two engineering degrees upon arrival but first worked as a busboy. Peter served in the US Air Force and is now a dentist. I was a journalist and am now in vocational ministry and a writer. We both are parents to our three amazing children, but he and I parent differently and relate differently to each child.

No one would try to convince us that because we are married or because we are both Korean American we are exactly the same and therefore should say the same things the same way. However, that is exactly what we are experiencing in our churches and in the United States today. As a Korean American immigrant woman who is married and the mother of three, I can't help but speak out against racism, sexism, xenophobia, and a host of other issues of injustice. This need to speak stems not only from my personal experiences but also from who I am and where I grew up—in proximity to people who experienced injustice. Even when I was in a place of privilege such as a private four-year university, I experienced what it was like to be a minority student while living with students far more privileged than me.

I can't teach the story of Queen Esther the same way a white man would because our minds and hearts encounter the story from such different starting points. I often have heard male pastors gloss over the selection of a new queen or portray it as an ancient version of the Miss Universe competition. Women are more likely to be aware of the sexual exploitation and power dynamics implicit in the story because we live in those same dynamics today. And as an immigrant woman of color, I have always been drawn to Esther's dual identity. I find that to be the core of the story, whereas someone from the majority culture may not dwell on that because they are the baseline for what is considered to be "normal." Our unity in Christ does not erase diversity. Our unity in Christ affirms and even demands diversity for the flourishing and stewarding of this world. Our diverse voices allow God's truth to be told in many ways.

PASSING AS ESTHER

If there were a book named after me, I would assume that most of the book would feature me, my words, and the details of my life. Perhaps that is indicative of how westernized I have become. But recently I noticed that we don't actually hear from Esther herself until four chapters into the book of Esther. Esther is silent for almost the entire first half of the book bearing her name.

What we do learn about Esther helps inform us and give shape to the voice we finally hear in chapter four. We learn that Esther is a foreigner. She is known by a different name in different circles—Hadassah is her Jewish name—so we can assume a level of assimilation to the majority culture. She has no family except for a male cousin who is in a position of authority and connected to power. And she is beautiful.

She's also not the only woman in this story. Before Esther is included in the narrative, we meet Queen Vashti, who is busy entertaining and tending to her own guests. When asked by King Xerxes to parade in front of him and his guests, Queen Vashti refuses. She asserts her own sense of self and uses her voice. In response, she is punished by being removed from her royal position lest other women in the kingdom start to assert themselves in active rebellion against the patriarchy. Sometimes, coming into ourselves requires entering into the pain and sacrifice of others who have gone before us.

After Queen Vashti is dethroned, Esther is selected from King Xerxes's harem as the new queen. Yet Esther is able to hide her nationality and family background from the king. Unlike Daniel, who continues to follow food restrictions and pray even after it has been outlawed, Esther doesn't stand out. People of color recognize what Esther is doing: she is passing; she is assimilating. The ability to assimilate includes many factors such as skin tone, education, social class, clothing, language acquisition, and vocabulary. Assimilation can be seen as selling out your cultural roots while simultaneously be required for survival.

I immigrated to the United States at eight months old, testing out my lungs for the benefit of my parents during the flight between Seoul, South Korea, and Seattle, Washington. I spoke only Korean until I started kindergarten. I used English to excel and fit in at school. I spoke Korean at home and church. For years, I hated my parents for "forcing" me to maintain some ability to speak, read, and write Korean. They were serious—they made their own language learning worksheets for me. Assimilating was necessary due to the teasing and sometimes physical harassment over what I couldn't control, such as my facial features, my last name, and the stereotypes. Ironically and understandably, my almost-grown children seek out connections to their Korean roots, whereas I wish I had stuck with the homemade worksheets and Korean folk dancing lessons, and wish I'd paid attention to my mom while she cooked. We don't know what regrets Esther may have had, but we do know that Mordecai instructed her to remain as Esther and not Hadassah, to not reveal her

Jewish heritage. As I get older I see both the wisdom and the failings in what Mordecai asked of Esther, and what my parents asked of me.

Before I was Kathy Khang, I was Khang KyoungAh, my Korean name given to me by my paternal grandfather. In Korean names, the first syllable or character is the family name or "last name." Unlike Western names that start by identifying the individual, many Eastern culture names begin with the family name because of the value of collective identity. Before *me* is *we.* The Chinese characters (Chinese because Korea was once occupied by the Chinese) for my given name means *congratulations* because I was the first girl born to my father's side of the family in four generations. My birth, a girl born into patriarchy, was celebrated. But that celebration and story got lost when we immigrated to America and I became Kathy. My parents had little hope that the American dream included people willing to learn the correct pronunciation of such a precious part of family history.

I read through five Bible commentaries and went through multiple Google searches to see if I could get an idea of what Jewish and Persian beauty standards were at the time of Esther, with no luck. But whatever those standards were, clearly Esther's beauty passed the test. My black female friends and I have talked about cultural preferences for lighter skin, so-called good hair, and other physical traits that are valued more than others. My Korean ancestors, with limited proximity to black or African people in a fairly homogenous country, valued light skin because darker skin was associated with the lower class, who usually worked outside as laborers and farmers.

Black women in the United States learned to hate their dark skin because it was the very thing that identified them as less than human in a country that saw fit to enslave Africans. The concept of passing is a racial one. Black women, unless they are very light-skinned and have so-called good hair, can't pass as white. As a Korean American with dark hair, a nose with an almost non-existent bridge, and eyes that are creased but differently so than my white friends, the only way I can pass into white American culture is to assume what privileges education and socioeconomic status can get me and downplay the differences.

So, much like Hadassah became Esther, I became Kathy. We both lost so much of our history and story, but in both cases it was a matter of survival and assimilation. The energy exerted to survive unfortunately can also mean connection to our communities gets weakened or lost. Esther, holed up in the king's harem pretending she isn't Jewish, loses touch with her community and has no idea that her people are facing destruction. Her limited privilege actually removes her from the community news. Esther adopts the rhythms of court life, probably eating whatever is put before her and perhaps not paying attention to the sounds announcing prayer. For me, trying desperately to become American meant distancing myself from what felt foreign in my life and clinging to any semblance of so-called whiteness—my name, not eating Korean food in public, being embarrassed of my parents' accents and use of Korean in public. My kids may have fewer inhibitions about taking Korean food to school, but their first names are still stereotypical white American names. Maybe

Mordecai hoped the same thing my parents hoped—that deep down inside, Esther and I would always know who we were and not be ashamed.

When Esther hears her uncle is wandering around in sack-cloth and ashes, she doesn't respond as a good Jewish woman who would understand that her uncle was acting that way out of mourning. Instead, she sends her servant to give him some "normal" clothes in hopes her uncle will stop. I just rolled my eyes at my parents and asked for a perm and designer jeans.

But at some point in our journey of losing and finding ourselves, we can hope that someone calls out our behavior and comes alongside us. The parts of our story that get lost or buried can only stay hidden for so long if we want to truly be whole and become who God created us to be. Esther has to choose who she will be. She has to recognize the parts she hid away and ignored. She has to come to terms with how her personal safety may not be what is at stake but something greater. When first presented with a copy of the edict outlining the genocide of the Jews and her uncle's request that she go to the king to beg for mercy, we hear Esther's voice in the story for the first time.

> All the king's officials and the people of the royal prov-inces know that for any man or woman who approaches the king in the inner court without being summoned the king has but one law: that they be put to death unless the king extends the gold scepter to them and spares their lives. But thirty days have passed since I was called to go to the king. (Esther 4:11)

She speaks like a Persian queen who knows the rules. She may even remember what happened to the last queen who dared to use her voice, when the king got rid of Vashti. But Mordecai doesn't back down and challenges her:

> Do not think that because you are in the king's house you alone of all the Jews will escape. For if you remain silent at this time, relief and deliverance for the Jews will arise from another place, but you and your father's family will perish. And who knows but that you have come to your royal position for such a time as this? (Esther 4:13-14)

This time, Esther hears the challenge and returns to her roots. She may not reclaim the name Hadassah, but she has come to grips with what she and her people are facing. Her response is to return to the Jewish ritual of fasting. When Esther asks all the Jews in Susa and her court attendants to fast with her, she reveals her Jewish identity.

USING YOUR POSITION

The summer before I went to college, I learned that I wasn't a US citizen. It was around the time I needed to update my passport in preparation for my first solo trip to South Korea. We learned that my green card had to be updated (the photo was of me as an eight-month-old baby), and I was given the option to apply for citizenship. I had assumed I was a citizen all my life and then suddenly found out that I wasn't actually an American citizen. I wasn't ready to make that decision—it was too confusing.

I opted to travel back to my homeland as a Korean citizen to see if I felt more at home there. I did and I didn't—because

I had returned as a Korean citizen but also as a Korean American, a *kyopo*. I didn't choose to pursue citizenship until 2010 when I was sworn in as a naturalized citizen of the United States. At that time, I realized that I had been speaking out more on issues of justice but lacked one privilege that was held by citizens: voting. In the naturalization process, I wrestled quite a bit with what giving up my Korean citizenship meant as well as the privilege of applying for and receiving US citizenship. What I had never considered was that as someone who was documented but not a citizen, I had chosen to sit on the sidelines. I had chosen silence in the political system. My friends called me out, asking why I thought voting didn't matter.

But I did think it mattered. And it mattered more and more as people were labeled as illegal. Politicians and even church leaders took sides, or worse, stayed silent on issues of immigration. For me, my royal position was one of comfortably sitting with my green card just outside the political fray inside the church until I learned that students I met were undocumented, that family friends were undocumented, that my sisters and brothers in Christ were undocumented.

Did I, like Esther, think that comfort meant protection? I felt like a fraud taking in all the information about politics—American and church politics—pontificating, opining, but never actually taking a risk by taking a stand for policy changes that might fail or have consequences. I did think that comfort meant protection, even though I knew in my heart that though my green card and Christian fluency protected me at a physical level, my soul would forever be affected by injustice and sin. Silence isn't always a privilege. Sometimes speaking out is dangerous and silence is a matter of self-preservation. But in this case, silence was a privileged response from someone who not only didn't vote but also opted out when the option was there.

For many of us, there are parts of our story we have just recently discovered or have known and kept to ourselves. Perhaps those are the stories that bring shame or embarrassment to our extended families—the abuse, the mental illness, the Klan member, the prison time, the lack of formal education, the unplanned pregnancy, the prescription drug addiction. We learn through Esther's experience that we can hide what isn't obvious to others, but our stories, known and unknown, have a deep impact on us. They connect us to one another. They shape our voice.

Esther could've spoken out against the genocide of the Jews without identifying herself as Jewish, but her voice is shaped dramatically because it is her story. She is able to connect deeply with her people's story of exile, homelessness, and persecution. She is able to reach into her personal story of a girl with no parents but with a people. Esther calls on her community and invites them into spiritual practices that are familiar: prayer and fasting. She is able to understand her place of privilege and vulnerability, and she speaks her truth to the king. She does not pretend to be a queen. She is a Persian Jewish queen speaking out on behalf of her Jewish people against the injustice they are facing. And she does that because she finally knows who she is.

When I cast my first vote, I did so fully aware that I had worked through the baggage and the blessing that come with being a hyphenated American and that there would probably be more to unpack in the future. But going to the polls that day with Peter didn't feel like I had lost a part of my identity or had given up my voice. It was truly the first time I remember being proud to be a Korean American naturalized citizen because I knew my journey out of silence had led me to the voting booth.

Esther knew she was still Hadassah. I knew I was still KyoungAh. I hope that you will come to know who you are as well.

Chapter 3

LEARNING TO SPEAK

I don't remember learning English, but apparently it was after I started kindergarten. I discovered this when my father told the story at my college graduation dinner. I graduated with a bachelor's degree in journalism and was heading north to Green Bay, Wisconsin, for a job with the daily newspaper as a consumer issues reporter. My father thanked the dinner guests for coming and uncharacteristically began to tear up as he spoke.

"I am so proud of our daughter who is going to be a journalist. A journalist. Our daughter who didn't know English when she started kindergarten is now going to be a writer," he said.

Wait a minute. What? I didn't know English when I started school?

Later, I vaguely recalled briefly sitting in an English as a Second Language class only to be moved out because my mother tongue was Korean, not Spanish. That memory made sense after I learned about my language acquisition journey.

Television shows such as *Sesame Street*, the *Electric Company*, and *ZOOM* were my English tutors.

The story of how and when I learned to speak English has shaped me and continues to shape me. Though my Korean is more broken and limited than ever, it's my heart language. I first learned hymns and the Lord's Prayer in Korean. Though I refer to my parents as my mother and father in this book, in life I use the Korean words *umma* and *abbah*. My younger sister never calls me Kathy and instead uses *un-nee*, the Korean word for a female's older sister. My husband didn't grow up using the Korean terms between siblings but wanted our children to grow up using them as a sign of endearment and respect, so now our children intersperse the terms with their given names. These words and customs are a way to instill values and tradition in our family.

My parents and I immigrated to the United States in 1971. My parents had a rudimentary grasp of written and spoken English when they immigrated, but it wasn't until the late 1980s when their mastery reached a new level. They had become small-business owners running a small dry cleaner in the west suburbs of Chicago. As they worked fourteen-hour days, six days a week through the years, countless interactions with customers helped my parents pick up enough language so that they could chitchat your ears off. The work was physically demanding, and my parents experienced an added level of exhaustion from having spent the day speaking English. I could see how being at our Korean church was not just a place of rest and restoration for the soul but also for the mind and body as prayers, hymns, and Scriptures were in their heart language. Even the food and drink served provided comfort and healing: barley tea, rich soups, and kimchi.

The concept of a heart language isn't built into US culture. The United States doesn't have an official language nor does it have an education system that encourages or values dual-language learning. It could be said that the only thing that connects people is that we all live in the same country—we don't all speak the same language, we're not all immigrants, and we're not all documented citizens. We don't even agree on what to call shoes used for physical activity: sneakers or gym shoes? For primary English-speakers in the United States, regional nuances and accents along with specific speech patterns and terms may evoke a feeling of connection and clarity. Perhaps the closest thing to a heart language is local or regional colloquialisms such as soda versus pop, sneakers versus gym shoes versus tennis shoes, water fountains versus bubblers.

There is power, emotion, and memory evoked in language. And Scripture invites us to understand how language has the power to destroy but also to heal and build. In the story of Esther, the decree announcing the destruction of the Jews is written out "in the script of each province and in the language of each people" (Esther 3:12). Heart language is used to hurt people. Yet later in Revelation, heart language is part of the gift we ultimately will receive:

> After this I looked, and there before me was a great multitude that no one could count, from every nation, tribe, people and *language*, standing before the throne and before the Lamb. They were wearing white robes

and were holding palm branches in their hands. And they cried out in a loud voice:

> "Salvation belongs to our God,
>   who sits on the throne,
>   and to the Lamb." (Revelation 7:9-10,
>   emphasis added)

It's a powerful, breathtaking image—a crowd so big that you can't count it, but you can grasp that the visible and audible distinctions and differences are a beautiful, valuable thing. We don't know exactly what those languages are, yet we know what they are saying. They are praising God. Amazing. I can only hope that in heaven I will be able to speak both Korean and English.

BABY STEPS

Learning to speak up doesn't necessarily mean primarily using spoken or written words. We first learn to communicate non-verbally. We have primal needs and desires, and we're wired to let the world know we exist. Babies can't speak but they communicate when they cry, fuss, follow objects with their eyes, smile, and coo. None of this is done using words or by speaking any language. Babies find a way to let us know that they are hungry, tired, wet, gassy, or happy. In a sense, it's also about ego—a part of the developing mind sensing and adapting to the real world. We learn to use our voice because we're all created to integrate our beliefs and values into some sort of action.

The trick is that babies don't have a filter. They have no inhibitions nor do they understand that a particular pitch over a long period of time is grating to adult ears at three o'clock in the morning. There is no self-censoring, no imposter syndrome, and no punishment (hopefully) for babies who are just doing what babies do.

You and I are not babies, but we do have something in common with children. As we grow from babies to adults, we are in what psychologist Jean Piaget calls the formal operational stage of cognitive development between adolescence and adulthood.[1] This is when we wrestle with abstract concepts and test hypotheses as we go along. Through adulthood, we put concepts such as justice, equity, love, and grace through the ringer, seeing what that might look like in real life. Developmental psychologist James Fowler outlines six stages of faith, and stages three through six fall within the formal operational stage of Piaget's framework:

Stage Three: Synthetic-Conventional faith is when conforming to authority shapes religious identity, and conflicts with personal beliefs are avoided because they may reveal inconsistencies.

Stage Four: Individual-Reflective faith is a season of struggle and ownership of one's personal beliefs and feelings. There is an awareness and openness to the fact that there may be conflicts and inconsistencies.

Stage Five: Conjunctive faith may feel like a spiritual midlife crisis, where conflicts are not resolved with more absolute truths but with a more complex understanding of the inherited faith and a willingness to stand in the tension of paradox.

Stage Six: Universalizing faith, or what some traditions call "enlightenment," where personal faith is not a ruler by which to judge others or treat others depending on the other person's alignment or agreement with your own faith.[2]

The process of learning, discovering, and testing out your voice can't be separated from your cognitive and spiritual development. Conflicts are bound to happen when people at different stages of development are testing out their voices. Between infancy and adulthood there is a lot of maturing, gaining of skills, and making mistakes. This is an invitation for spiritual leaders—pastors, youth leaders, and mentors—to stay hopeful and to be kind as we are all on this journey. We are adults with our own broken sense of self-importance and ego. Some of us need to think less of ourselves while others need more confidence and support. All of us, however, are meant to be active participants in life and to encourage others to do the same. How will the world know we are Christians if our love is just a feeling and never compels us into action?

LEARNING TO SPEAK UP

Between infancy and adulthood, we mature, gain skills, and make mistakes. To learn how to speak up as adults, here are some questions to ask yourself and work through.

Who are you?

Know thyself and thy roots. In sociology this is called social location, which is defined by your gender, race, social class, age, ability, religion, sexual orientation, and geographic location.

This set of information places each person in a particular spot in community. We can mistakenly believe we are the center of the universe if we focus only on the words from Psalm 139:13-14: "For you created my inmost being; you knit me together in my mother's womb. I praise you because I am fearfully and wonderfully made." But we need to read those verses in the context of all of Scripture and time. We exist within the context of community.

How are you different from others? How are you unique? My husband and I are both Korean American, but our different immigration stories have shaped us in different ways. We live in a homogenous middle- to upper-middle-class suburb with friends who have been shaped by their experiences growing up in small rural towns or in working-class families.

Do you have a college degree? Did your parents? How far back can you trace your family's roots? What does that say about who you are? Are you a racial or ethnic minority, and if so, how did that affect your childhood experiences at school and in your neighborhood? How does that affect your life as an adult at work and home? If you are of the majority racial or ethnic group, how has that affected your experiences?

I grew up hearing about North Korea in pejorative terms in reference to its regime and sometimes its people. As a child, I learned in world history classes that North Korea was the communist enemy. Both of Peter's parents have roots in North Korea from before the armistice that divided the peninsula. After we were married, I realized that I had some prejudiced attitudes against a people and country I actually had ties to that ran deeper than artificial boundaries. It doesn't mean we don't condemn violent and dangerous political regimes and their leaders, but it does mean I check myself before making fun of or speaking negatively about North Koreans. It also forces me to think more critically and deeply about injustice globally.

It's worth mentioning that we all have a culture and history, and that includes white people. Pastor Daniel Hill assumed that as a white man, he had no culture. He stated as much during a sincere exchange with one his best friends, who is South Asian/Indian. His friend responded, "Daniel, you may be white, but don't let that lull you into thinking you have no culture. White culture is very real. In fact, when white culture comes in contact with other cultures, it almost always wins. So it would be a really good idea for you to learn about your culture."[3]

We are all children of God, and diversity is part of that unity—not conformity or assimilation. Knowing who you are helps you deal with all of the different people you will meet, especially during those times when you're speaking out or challenging them. Knowing who you are also helps you recognize everyone else's humanity.

What is in your wheelhouse?

What issues do you care most deeply about? Identify what compels you to speak up. What people, problems, dreams, and values are near and dear to your heart? What things make you angry and question humanity? Where do you find hope? Take a look at what charities you support—this will help you recognize issues you care about enough to give sacrificially by putting your money where your mouth is. Another thing to consider is what issue is pulling at your heart and soul so much that it might make you do something you never thought you'd do?

An example of this in my own life is when I attended the National Women's March on Washington in January 2017, where millions of women gathered in solidarity not just in Washington, DC, but also in cities across the globe. This wave of activism demanded my attention as it gained momentum nationwide. At first, I was hesitant to go because the event came under its fair share of criticism, including an accusation of a glaring lack of diversity and a lack of a clear goal while in the beginning stages of organizing. Women of color throughout the United States, myself included, also hesitated to go all-in with a demonstration taking place *after* the election because we believed this kind of outrage and call to action *before* the election could have rendered a different election result all together. But I chose to go—not only because I had the privilege of having the time and means to travel to Washington, DC, but also because it was an opportunity to take a road trip with my daughter, Bethany, and my close friend Tina. Traveling twelve hours each way together gave us a lot of time to listen to each other's stories.

It was not something any of us would normally do. Bethany, Tina, and I aren't drawn to demonstrating, public protests, or gathering in close proximity outdoors with thousands of strangers. But we decided that marching for women's rights was important. Tina and I also had friends who cared about women's rights but didn't feel the need to drop everything and march. It wasn't their thing, and that's okay. Shortly after the march, Tina invited several of us to join her in a postcard writing campaign to our representatives in Congress and other politicians. It was a perfect example of how there are different ways to engage in the causes in your wheelhouse.

Are you willing to fail or be judged?

I am in awe of my older son, Corban. During his senior year in high school, he decided to go out with a bang by joining the gymnastics team, even though he had never even taken so much as a tumbling class. The team was no-cut, meaning anyone who was committed to giving his best effort at practice would have a spot on the team but not necessarily on the competition roster. Corban started getting ready a few weeks before the season by working out, drinking protein shakes, and practicing handstands. He came home from practice one afternoon with a cut on his lip and a gash on his right shin. When I asked him how practice went, he answered, "I am broken." Apparently, he was attempting some sort of fancy roll or flip and managed to hit his knee with his lip. He had also tried something on the parallel bars and his right leg didn't clear the bar. As he gave me the details complete with sound effects and gestures, he was smiling, even though he was describing his utter failure. I was so encouraged by his willingness to try something completely new at a time in life when taking risks may come with a social cost, especially if you might literally fall on your face or bottom.

Speaking up, even testing out your voice, requires resilience. It's not a matter of toughening up, becoming immune, or being unmoved by criticism or failure. It's a matter of humility. Are you willing to learn from failure? How will you respond to critics?

More than a decade ago, a prominent Christian publishing house used inaccurate and unhelpful Asian stereotypes for its annual vacation Bible school (VBS) curriculum. When a Korean American pastor and professor went public with his concerns, critics brushed him off as being too sensitive about irrelevant ethnic and racial issues. Others joined his single voice of concern, criticizing and increasing awareness of how negative racial and ethnic stereotypes are used in both Christian and mainstream media to deliver the gospel message to young children in this case. This was the first public social media campaign I joined. I had to speak up as I imagined how awful it would be for young children across the country to be introduced to Jesus by mostly non-Asian American church volunteers wearing a hodgepodge of "Asian-themed" attire and holding chopsticks (did you know that not all Asian countries use chopsticks?). It was the first time I received emails and face-to-face comments from people who told me I was being too sensitive, prioritizing my ethnic identity over my Christian identity, or that I was a reverse racist (that's not a thing). It left me a little bruised and more aware of what it meant to use my voice and face harsh criticism and critique. It took almost ten years before the company president, who wasn't even with the company when the VBS curriculum was published, publicly apologized at a large national conference for church leaders.

What are your unique gifts, talents, and skills?

How did God design you to communicate with others? Not everyone is called to be a writer or a community developer, but everyone is called to do something and be present.

Looking back, I can see how God had been nudging and shaping my daughter, Bethany, to understand her skills as a dancer and use them an outlet to share women's stories with honor and respect. Over time, she learned that her skills didn't fit classical ballet. By the time she was ready to go *en pointe*, it was obvious she didn't have the best "turnout" or the rotation of the legs from the hips. Her knees or her hips were never where they were supposed to be even though her feet were. She learned in college that she was blessed with an anterior pelvic tilt. Her body and heart would be in modern dance.

But it wasn't just about learning steps and performing. Bethany wanted to tell stories in her choreography. Two of her dance pieces in high school focused on young women examining and struggling to claim and define their identity. She effectively used lighting and costuming. She even named of one of her pieces "(Me)dicine," a take on the song title but also on her vision for the piece. It wasn't until recently that I made the connection that Bethany's desire to attend the Women's March on Washington was another way she wanted to connect her body to her passions and talents in a different way—by marching rather than dancing.

Another artist using her skills in a unique way is Ellie Yang Camp, a calligrapher and lettering artist based in Mountain View, California. Camp has always had an activist side and is passionate about racial issues, which are personal to her as an Asian American woman. However, she had never made the connection between her art and her personal voice because calligraphy is a literal art that often represents someone else's words. When Camp realized that she wanted to do more than just make the words of stories look beautiful on paper, she landed on the idea of paper cranes, something she and other Asian American women grew up doing almost as absent mindedly as doodling. Originating in Japanese culture, paper cranes are a symbol of healing and hope. She launched The Crane Project, a conceptual art project where Camp takes painful stories and microaggressions experienced by women of color and writes them in calligraphy with black sumi ink on white origami paper. It's then folded into a beautiful paper crane. Camp said, "The liturgical process of reflecting, writing, and folding is meant to give a literal representation of transformation of pain into beauty."[4]

Another example of someone using their skills is Reesheda N. Graham-Washington, an entrepreneur and executive director at Communities First Association, a national, faith-based organization committed to community transformation through asset-based community development. Washington, a former Chicago charter school principal and teacher, saw an opportunity to invest in the community by opening a coffee shop that also would serve as a space for local artists and community dialogue as well as an opportunity to use her leadership skills in a new way. L!VE Café in Chicago features chairs and tables created by local artisans, employs people from the community, and serves as host to community events, book clubs, and lectures on topics ranging from vintage clothing to black presence in television.[5]

Raising Her Voice

When Reesheda N. Graham-Washington, executive director of Communities First Association, learned to use her voice, she changed her vocation.[a]

Question: What made you decide to leave education and move full-time into community development work?

Answer: I had started to wonder if what I was doing to impact education was even impactful at all. I wondered whether or not the work I was doing, particularly in education administration, had any impact on students. But what I knew to be true was that the community was having an impact on students, whether the impact was positive or negative. To see the direct outcome in the lives of students as a result of the communities they lived in compelled me to dream about what would happen if communities were being positioned, resourced, and supported in ways that bolstered positive experiences for students. My theory was that if we enhance the quality of community that students were engaging in and experiencing, over time the positive impact would inform who the student was becoming more holistically and, as a result, would impact their education.

Q: How has your voice developed and changed as you have made the shift from educator to community developer to entrepreneur?

A: When I left the field of education, I left quite a few things behind. I left behind an assessment system that stifled the creativity and voices of educators; I left behind a system that did not value the expertise of people of color in educating students of color. I moved into a space in the community where the language I was speaking in a lot of ways was already understood. Consequently, my voice was bigger. I felt like I had more of a profound voice and means to impact the lives of the communities that I serve alongside. I also felt like there was a level of depth to what I could speak into because the work of community development is much more holistic than focusing my time and attention into one system (the education system). Rather than waiting for space at the table, I started to see the urgency of the mandate for voices like mine as it pertains to entrepreneurship because I see the power that lies in having people see someone who look likes me and sounds like me do the work of community development. It frees them to do that same kind of work around economic development and entrepreneurship.

My voice is much stronger, and that may have something to do with the fact that I have been out of the field of education for almost a decade now. As I get older, I feel a greater sense of urgency to use my voice in a way that creates liberation for others, but I'm also aware that the landscape and community development and entrepreneurship affords me more opportunities to use my voice prophetically than when I worked in the system of education.

Q: Are there issues about which you have found yourself becoming more vocal or active in using your voice? If so, why? What has changed?

A: I have definitely found myself being more vocal and active around issues of equity because I feel like the issue of equity touches every other issue, challenge, concern, and need for transformation that we have in our country and in our world. I believe what has changed is my own willingness to speak prophetically and to forego people's acceptance of me or my values and beliefs. I am now willing to compromise my comfort and my relationships in order to make room for the imperatives for all people in all systems, always.

Q: What advice do you have for people who may not see themselves as activists but want to grow in integrating their values into their profes-sional and community life?

A: In my book *Soul Force: Seven Pivots to Courage, Community, and Change*, I talk about the reality that the movement will occur when each of us is willing to integrate our values into our professional and community lives. The reality is that what is required is the development of a posture of humility, such that we can learn from one another that which we do not already know about ourselves and about our communities. This kind of transformation will also require our willingness to make changes to who we are and how we show up to each other in times of challenge, even when we are afraid. Rather than waiting for our fear to pass, we must be willing to make small yet courageous steps toward the unfamiliar. We must simply be willing to "do it afraid."

[a]*From personal correspondence with the author, October 11, 2017.*

Who are your people?

Learning to speak in the context of community is key for the long haul. We operate out of our individual skill sets and passions, but God modeled community in the way we were created, with God the Father, Son, and Holy Spirit together and in partnership creating humankind in God's image. We were intended to flourish and fill the earth together.

Community can be the cheerleader and the springboard from where you find your courage as an individual to speak. You find solidarity and identify with the people in your community. Even if you come from a Western culture that emphasizes individualism, press into your faith and the biblical examples of Moses, Esther, and Jesus, who all lived in and leaned on different communities.

I think I'm an awesome singer but people who have heard me sing tell me otherwise. We may have an idea of what we enjoy doing, but we need to be humble and willing in seeking out others who will give us helpful feedback and coaching. Corban didn't know what he was doing when he agreed to join the gymnastics team. He just knew he wanted to be with some of his closest friends. So instead of asking me, his biggest fan, he asked his friends Joe and Jacob who actually are gymnasts about how to prepare. Corban trained with them in the preseason, and they told Corban he needed to strengthen his arms, develop his core, and gain some weight. Corban, a cross-country runner, had the athletic skills, but he needed gymnasts and coaches to identify his best skills.

There is a chance that your community will experience tension and confusion as you experiment with raising your voice. Both Asian American and white friends, some of whom encouraged me to write and speak publicly, have told me that I've become too outspoken on matters of injustice and that my speaking out only increases division. Speaking up doesn't increase division. It brings injustice and sin to the forefront. Speaking up can be an avenue of truth and healing, which can be painful for you and your friends.

With the advent of blogging and social media, the majority of people I met believed that in order to use their voice they needed to start a blog—no editor required. Blogging hasn't died, but the days of viral blogs or blog posts in its original form are over. You can go viral with a meme or Twitter post, but using your voice isn't a one-time event.

The collision between social media and the emergence of Christian celebrities is an interesting one. Let's be really honest here. How many of us Christian bloggers and writers have imagined writing that one blog everyone reads? And then getting invited to speak at that conference everyone talks about? Oh, no? Me neither.

Ambition is not a dirty word. However, we need to have strong community around us to help discern our gifts. Sometimes community will give you the confidence. Sometimes community will help check our egos. Activist Deray McKesson tweeted, "I found my voice when I lost my ego."[6]

What diverse voices are you learning from?

Be informed and learn from people who are different than you. The internet can actually be a time suck. I find myself mindlessly spending hours, yes, hours during the course of a week, and yes, you do too (if you are honest), on Facebook, Twitter, Instagram, while Voxing, Snapchatting, and texting. Spending time online makes us believe we have gotten to know people better and know lots of important things, but we actually come away with very little knowledge or understanding. My social-media world and my real-life world can quickly become echo chambers of posts and people who think exactly like I do and believe similar things if I am not intentional.

Walk away from the screen. Commit to reading books by authors of color, particularly theologians and Christian leaders of color (like this one). Commit to reading books by authors who have a different viewpoint on issues than you do or come from a different racial, ethnic, or socioeconomic experience than you do. Think about the podcasts and subjects you are most interested in and then add a few from the "least interested" pile. If you are a man, listen to women preach. If you are a woman, listen to women preach. And don't limit your consumption to Western voices. There is an entire world out there. Take a hard look at your circle of friends and be honest about the diversity reflected in your relationships. And then take your questions, along with what you are learning, back to the spaces you can influence and use your voice.

How do you care for yourself?

Steward your gifts and your self. Being a Monday-morning quarterback doesn't take a lot of effort. That's why so many of us do it. Being fully engaged in the world requires energy and rest. It's often referred to as self-care.

I write this from a specific social location. I'm a woman of color. These are trying, difficult times. I know that some people turn to Facebook as a place of joy and avoiding hard things. Others use it to post about their emotions or to process pain. Some are lurkers who read but never engage, while others are fast and effusive with their comments and likes. There also are those who have both left Facebook and social media or who never entered those spaces. However, very few of us can completely disconnect from the 24/7 flow of news and noise—television, cable, radio, computers, GPS watches, and smart-phones have changed our environment. Even some of the least social-media-connected people I know have longed for the "good old days." Some of my friends wish for the days of "nice" social media with cat memes and news about everyone else's perfect families, but my feed has never been void of politics, challenging news, religious commentary, and the occasional crockpot or pressure cooker recipe.[7] For me, social media was never about escapism, but I think it was for some people. Now, things are hitting closer to home or politics and policies are finally hitting you in a new way, and you're exhausted. For others, like myself, we have been exhausted for a very long time.

But we weren't designed to stay in a state of perpetual exhaustion and anxiety. God did not spend a metaphorical six days on creating to spend the seventh day fretting. We need to care for ourselves—physically, spiritually, emotionally, mentally, and psychologically—not only to fight against oppression and injustice but also to simply be. Our healthy whole selves are meant to be a testimony to God's goodness even in times such as these (especially in times such as these). God wants to use our healthy selves as we wake up to the reality that there are people and forces who don't want us, particularly people of color, immigrants, and the LGBTQIA community.

Self-care isn't about spa treatments and weekend getaways, though those are *amazing* if you can afford them. Self-care isn't about avoiding or numbing the pain. If I find myself roaming resale shops and the sale racks with no purpose, I know that I'm just trying to avoid dealing with my pain. Self-care is restorative and preparatory. Remember the year of beauty treatments Queen Esther had in Esther 2:12? I wonder if that year also helped prepare her to lead her people. Audre Lorde said, "Caring for myself is not self-indulgence, it is self-preservation, and that is an act of political warfare."[8] I think of self-care in the following three categories.

Rest. Many of us are walking around sleep-deprived. I'm not talking about parents with infants or young children. I'm talking about all of us.[9] We are also bombarded with information and glowing screens all the time, even the kiddos. Screen time isn't restful. A recent unscientific study of my friends' Facebook posts showed an uptick of people feeling more stressed and anxious from social media and wanting to take breaks. We need to rest. Remember, God rested on day seven. Things to do for straight-up rest include

- Go to bed before midnight. Lately I have been shooting for seven hours of sleep. (My kids are in their early twenties and late teens, so I often find reasons to be up late worrying.)

- Take short naps. If you don't nap, can you grab a catnap on the train? Before you drive into rush-hour traffic?

- Turn off technology. Technology is my nemesis. I need to be better at getting off of my phone or computer at least one hour before I go to bed. Anyone want to be my accountability partner?

- Limit caffeine and alcohol. I tried cutting off caffeine at 3 p.m., but that wasn't my problem. It's the glass of wine with the evening news that doesn't help with sleep.

Restore. Feeling refreshed and restored is different than just getting enough sleep. I think of rest as turning off my engine. Restoration is filling my tank. I recommend the following:

- Exercise. My favorites are walking, yoga, and kickboxing. Walking gets me outside in the fresh air. It gets me out of my head and, if I'm alone, it's my time to rant with Jesus. Yoga has helped me connect my body awareness to my breathing. Kickboxing is great cardio, and I like to hit the bag. I have the privilege of being able to afford a gym membership, but before that happened, I spent a lot of time walking and doing squats in my kitchen. I have also bartered my services as an editor for a personal training session.

- Take care of your mental health. My tank needs ten milligrams of Lexapro a day to treat anxiety and depression. There's no shame in it. My brain needs a daily adjustment. If you think you might have mental health issues, *go see your doctor* and make sure all your levels are where they need to be. Last year, I was worried I was falling into a deeper depression, so I called my doctor. After running tests, it turned out I was anemic.

- Spend time in community. When I am in a funk, the last thing I want to do is go out, but it is often the thing I need to get myself out of myself. Invite friends over for dessert. Take lunch to a friend. Talk with other people. If you're an introvert, you can spend time with people who love you and don't expect you to process externally.

Be ready to go. This isn't about spa treatments. This is about taking care of yourself because it's not just about you. What is God inviting you to do, to become? I think of President Barack Obama's chant, "Fired up? Ready to go!" I think of Jesus telling the disciples, "Therefore go and make disciples of all

nations" (Matthew 28:19) or the angel telling the women at
the tomb, "Come and see . . . go quickly and tell" (Matthew 28:6-7).
Our beautiful, strong minds are meant to *go*. How will you be
ready? This is how I feed my heart, soul, and mind:

- Read. Do the work of feeding your mind. Read authors
  who have a different political-bent or point of view. Read
  authors of color. Read fiction and non-fiction. Read poetry
  and young adult novels. Listen to audiobooks and podcasts if you don't have the time to sit and read. (But
  remember, we always have time for the things we make
  time for.) Read the Bible.

- Use both sides of your brain. View art, attend performances (local high schools and community colleges are
  a great resource for affordable options), listen to music,
  and then make art, journal, and dance to the music.
  Using your voice takes work, but it should come from a
  place of love and joy.

- Pray. Pray alone. Pray in community. Learn to pray new
  prayers and in new ways. Pray aloud and silently. Write
  your prayers. Walk your prayers. Breathe your prayers.

PUTTING IT INTO PRACTICE

When I met Diana, she was in crisis. She was a leader working
through some significant team dynamics and conflict, and she
felt like she didn't have the energy, permission, or ability to
talk about what she was experiencing or to ask questions
about leadership, specifically about her leadership as a young
woman of color. Diana continued to develop student leaders

who valued her leadership and mentoring, but she also needed a community to support her as she examined her identity and calling and sought potential leadership opportunities in a system that was flawed. Diana attended seminary, served as a leader, and completed some projects that were a stretch for her. When her gifts as a preacher were affirmed, she continued to lean on her mentors and friends to make sure she was resting, asking better questions, and finding opportunities to teach and preach. Her mentors and friends encouraged her to apply for grants and jobs just for the experience and then write about the experience. She learned that she hates writing but loves teaching.

As Diana became more confident in who she was and in her skills, she said yes to speaking opportunities. She intentionally mentored other young women of color and created a space for female faculty of color. Diana leaned into her own experience of pain and found her voice for her own sake and then realized what she had learned was vitally important to share with other gifted women of color. Diana was my cheerleader as I wrestled with some of my writing and editing. When speaking about Diana with a young woman, that woman told me she had recently attended an event coordinated and taught by Diana. She said Diana's leadership and teaching were powerful and transformative. A decade ago, Diana could barely talk about the conflicts she was processing. Now, she's speaking with her own voice and creating space for people to do the same thing.

Chapter 4

FEAR AND FAILURE

I have spent my whole life (minus eight months) in the Midwest, where we have a phrase that guides our interpersonal communications and interactions. We call it *Midwest nice*, which means a superficial collegiality with a touch of passive aggressiveness. We smile and nod and appear to be in complete agreement even if we disagree with what you are saying. We may dismiss everything you've just said with a simple "Oh." Author and professor Soong-Chan Rah once said that Midwest nice is like "a dog that licks your face while peeing on your shoes."[1] Midwest nice means that we may not disagree—but don't assume our silence means agreement. We are taught to keep the peace, which is perfect for me as a Korean American whose cultural roots also value harmony of the community over the opinions and desires of an individual.

What has been strange is to see how Midwest nice can also be mistaken as godliness—pursuing superficial peace over costly justice. Somewhere along the way, the subversive, dangerous message of the gospel that invites people to live like a man who hung out with people in the margins has given way to a nice Christian faith that creates a false dichotomy: unity versus diversity. We wrongly believe that unity means conformity and assimilation, and in order to be unified we must agree to disagree, silence the dissenters and prophets, and be nice rather than challenge the status quo.

We start by recognizing the ways culture silences us. We move to understanding how God created us to be communicators in a variety of ways and find our identity and voice. In order to effectively use our voice, we need to walk and speak humbly. Much like learning to walk, we will need to overcome our fears and address our failures.

GROWING INTO YOUR VOICE

Believe it or not, I didn't always speak out. I had my opinions and could articulate my values, but I also was very aware of what kept me from using my voice: I was afraid. On Facebook I have no shame sharing how I feel about today's news, but very few people in my neighborhood follow me on social media. Those who do follow me know *exactly* what I'm thinking or reading or eating. But that wasn't always the case, and it didn't have anything to do with social media—it had to do with the fear I experienced while I was learning how to have conviction, wisdom, and a vision beyond myself.

Our children had the privilege of attending a good, local public elementary school. It's the oldest elementary school in the district, and parents are involved (maybe too involved) in maintaining its educational excellence as well as its traditions. One tradition is the Pilgrim Celebration featuring pilgrims and Native Americans from the first Thanksgiving. Adorable second-graders dress up like pilgrims, and the parents—in what is supposed to be a surprise for the kids but never is because the school has been doing this for decades—dress up as Native Americans. The first Thanksgiving didn't actually happen this way, but it makes for a great tradition and photo opportunities.[2]

Parents show up wearing a variety of generic, culturally appropriating, and sometimes offensive Halloween costumes, even though the real story involves a specific tribe called the Wampanoag. The first time I attended the celebration, I honestly can't remember what I wore with my jeans under my black coat. I know I brought a wool blanket to use as a shawl. Our children greeted us by presenting us with a headband decorated with construction paper feathers. The awkwardness of seeing my neighbors in their versions of "Indian" costumes, some complete with face paint and feathers, was made worse by one of the mothers wearing what could best be described as a "sexy Pocahontas" costume. I could see everyone looking at her, and I did what any brave person would do at the first sign of slut shaming—I said nothing to them. Instead, I walked over and started talking with her. I didn't know what else to do.

One would hope that this was as awkward as it would get, but it got worse. A parent volunteer, dressed in a generic headdress and "Native American" warrior costume, came out as Chief Massasoit. He wore face paint and spoke in halted

English, mimicking what he interpreted as a native Wampanoag accent. I was mortified. And I did nothing.

I actually did nothing again when I attended the Pilgrim Celebration for my son Elias. When I went to the event for the second time, I didn't bring my wool blanket and I tried explaining cultural appropriation to him. I didn't say anything to a teacher or an administrator. I just talked with our son and tried to distract him from paying attention to Chief Massasoit. It was all I had the courage to do because I was afraid that if I brought up race and cultural appropriation at the event, it would somehow affect my children at school. I didn't want to be *that* parent—the Asian American mom who complained about a beloved school tradition tinged with racism and bad history.

Sometimes we lack the courage to act, even as we wrestle with the conviction.

THE INJUSTICE WE DO NOT UNDERSTAND

We often stay silent and do nothing by convincing ourselves the offense isn't actually that offensive. Sometimes we don't speak up because the injustice doesn't affect our daily lives. We don't understand the impact of a law or the injustice inflicted on others because it doesn't impact the people closest to us or it isn't a matter of our heart or heart language.

Queen Esther may have been able to avoid getting involved if it wasn't for the actions of her uncle Mordecai. In Esther 3, when the king ordered all royal officials to kneel before Haman the Agagite, Mordecai refused. There is a passing mention that others in the king's court knew Mordecai was Jewish, but it's unclear whether Mordecai's refusal was a religious or personal protest. Regardless, Haman was offended by Mordecai's behavior and blamed all the Jews, not just Mordecai. Haman asked the king to issue a decree to have the Jews destroyed. The royal secretaries were summoned, and they made sure the message was clearly communicated:

> They wrote out in the script of each province and in the language of each people all Haman's orders to the king's satraps, the governors of the various provinces and the nobles of the various peoples. . . . A copy of the text of the edict was to be issued as law in every province and made known to the people of every nationality so they would be ready for that day. (Esther 3:12, 14)

In response to the decree, Mordecai persuaded Esther to appeal to the king on behalf of all the Jews. Esther became invested in seeking justice because it affected her personally.

At the Pilgrim Celebration, when I saw that many of the parents were judging the woman who was dressed inappropriately, I had *just* enough courage to go stand with her because I know what it feels like to be judged by my appearance. I've been the focus of teasing, bullying, and sexualization my entire life due to my physical characteristics as a Korean American woman. I stood with the woman, not because I was Native American or had friendships with Native Americans who could've told me about the pain and danger of stereotypes, but because I had faced similar situations. I knew in my gut that stereotyping and racist depictions of the Wampanoag people was wrong. So why wasn't that enough for me to speak up to the teachers in charge of the event? At the time, the offense didn't cut to my heart deep enough to compel me to act. But now I realize that we can't wait to act until we are personally affected by something. If we wait to have a personal interaction with everyone of a different ethnicity, gender, sexual orientation, and so on before we act or speak up against injustice, it will take an eternity.

A good and painful example of this is the #BlackLivesMatter movement that emerged in 2013.[3] It was started by three black women in response to the acquittal of George Zimmerman in the fatal shooting of Trayvon Martin, a black teenager. It seemed that an armed adult man's sense of safety was valued more than Martin's life, and people publically questioned on both social media and in their communities whether or not black lives mattered. The movement gained traction in 2014 with the police shooting of Michael Brown in Ferguson, Missouri, and the choking death of Eric Garner in New York City. Anger, pain, and a call to action spilled out into the streets. Protesters demanded the public take notice.

As things in New York City and Ferguson were percolating, I was on sabbatical after fifteen years in vocational ministry. I was supposed to be resting and recovering, dreaming about what might happen professionally and personally in my next chapter of life, as well as asking God for a burning bush of clarity. Instead I found myself unable to turn away from the news coverage of the violence against black women and men— not because I was in similar danger but because I was and had been purposefully listening to black friends and colleagues who had lived and were still living this experience.

As a Korean American woman, I have learned to expect to be catcalled or to be on the receiving end of racist, sexist epithets. It doesn't matter where I am—in the city, at an airport, or in my neighborhood. It's usually in city settings where men of any and all skin colors think it's fine to say to me, "Hello, lady! Why don't you give me a smile?" and expect me to respond in kind. I don't. Greeting me with "*Konnichiwa!*" is also unwelcome and not likely to get a positive response. I spent most of my childhood in the suburbs and can still remember the bullies, even in high school, who didn't like the way this so-called "chink" looked, stood, or breathed.

I grew up with a healthy suspicion of police officers, but when I got pulled over in 1993 for the first time because I was speeding just south of Green Bay, Wisconsin, I never feared for my life. In fact, I wondered if the officer and I would recognize each other because I was a local newspaper reporter at the time. My parents never warned me about interactions with law enforcement. They also never considered calling the police when rocks were thrown through our window or trash was thrown on our yard.

I was unnerved as I watched the Ferguson situation unfold on the news; Michael Brown's body laid on the hot pavement for hours. It was heartbreaking and frightening. I felt it deeper than I had in previous similar situations because I was also following the reactions on social media of my black and brown friends and colleagues—people I didn't have earlier in my life. The racism of the situation was familiar, but their specific experiences and context were new to me. Through their own deep pain, anger, and fear, they were teaching me a new language and framework to understand racial injustice. I more clearly understood the unjust laws and rules, written and unspoken, that affected their lives. I began to understand those edicts—defined by skin color—that had been written against and for them and their communities, just as I had learned to understand similar injustices that were reserved for Asian Pacific Islanders. You learn to understand injustice and be better prepared to speak about it when you are immersed in it.

It's no coincidence that there was an uptick in addressing racism, sexism, and faith in my social media presence and when I spoke in public. The more I read books by authors of color, the more I listened to my Asian and Asian American, Latino, Native, and black and brown friends and colleagues, and the more I was willing to make mistakes and understand points of connection between "them" and "us," the more clear the injustice became.

LET GOD TAKE CARE OF IT

One way to deal with our discomfort with disagreement is to silence ourselves and others. We preserve the status quo by blaming God. We say, "God is in control," or "Let God and let go." Well, yes and no. God is God. God is in control. But God isn't micromanaging our every movement and detail as a puppeteer, even though God is aware of it all. Being a Jesus-follower, trusting in God's sovereignty, and believing in our hearts that God is in control doesn't absolve us from taking action or speaking out against injustice. In fact, it should be a reminder for us to take the risk and speak up in our churches and communities. Our churches should be leading us to raise our voices.

Esther and Mordecai wrestled with a sense of community and a sense of personal and communal responsibility. When Mordecai and the Jews learned of the edict, they did what you do when you learn that your people are in harm's way— they mourned by fasting, weeping, and wailing. Many of them, including Mordecai, put on physical signs of mourning by wearing sackcloth and ashes.

This goes back to understanding injustice as something beyond a personal offense. The entire Jewish population had a universal way to communicate its grief and fear in response to the king's edict. Esther's attendant, who presumably is not Jewish, tells her about Mordecai wearing sackcloth and ashes. Esther's response is a personal, one-on-one message back to her uncle to find out what's troubling him. It never occurs to her that it could involve her community. Esther learns that this is something that goes beyond the two of them, and when Mordecai first asks for help, she defers to the letter of the law. Approaching the king without first being summoned puts Esther at risk of death.

Mordecai's response back to Esther is aptly used as a contemporary rallying cry for people to rise up and speak up, and rightly so. However, it's also a reminder that God is in control even as God invites individuals into community with one another in shared humanity *and* to speak up.

Do not think that because you are in the king's house you alone of all the Jews will escape. For if you remain silent at this time, relief and deliverance for the Jews will arise from another place [God is in control], but you and your father's family will perish. And who knows but that you have come to your royal position for such a time as this [but this doesn't absolve you or your family from acting]? (Esther 4:12-14)

Our individual comfort and safety should always be at risk if we are living out the gospel. When Jesus asks if we are willing to take up the cross, it isn't a comfortable, custom-fit cross with memory foam and cotton sheets. The invitation is to risk safety and comfort, risk fitting in, and risk friendships, even if we don't have all of the privileges this world offers. We know that being citizens of heaven doesn't excuse us from participating in taking action and speaking up in places that bring about awareness and change, even when it means you step on a few toes of privilege and comfort. How can we pray, "Your kingdom come, your will be done on *earth* as it is in heaven" without recognizing this is an invitation to raise our voices?

SILENCE SERVES ME AND PROVIDES COVER

The reason I most often choose to stay silent is the one I don't want to admit. If I benefit from the status quo, I have a vested interest in maintaining it. Silence is complicity. Speaking out is often labeled as rocking the boat or causing trouble, but silence is just as dangerous.

I felt uncomfortable at the Pilgrim Celebration, but no one was questioning my right to be there. No one aggressively demanded an explanation for the lack of effort behind my costume. I belonged as long as I didn't publicly raise my concerns about cultural appropriation and racism. I stayed silent for another few years, until my youngest son had moved on from that school, before I sent an email to the principal about my concerns. I waited until there would be no connection between me, the "complaining parent," and my son Elias. I regret staying silent for so long in regards to something that could've been better addressed by a parent with a vested interest in changing things. I would like to believe that I would have said something if the school held an offensive Lunar New Year celebration, but that doesn't grant me much solace. I sit in grace.

Remember that for future reference, by the way. We will make mistakes whether or not we choose to speak out.

My favorite example in the Bible of someone who makes this kind of mistake is Peter. He is eager to please, and when Jesus speaks to his disciples about his death and resurrection, Peter is there with the perfect response:

> "Even if all fall away on account of you, I never will."
>
> "Truly I tell you," Jesus answered, "this very night, before the rooster crows, you will disown me three times."
>
> But Peter declared, "Even if I have to die with you, I will never disown you." (Matthew 26:33-35)

However, Peter goes on to do exactly what Jesus said he would. Peter doesn't speak up as a faithful follower of Jesus and denies Jesus three times. He doesn't speak up until confronted by Jesus. Imagine if Peter let that whopper of a failure stop him from taking action to share the good news. Imagine how the church would've been affected by Peter's silence. And also consider what might have happened to Peter if he let his failure define him instead of living in the truth he experienced with Jesus.

Fear of failure can silence us for a long time. About a decade ago, I supervised a staff team of six gifted and strong personalities. Through a series of failures on my part to communicate expectations and provide clear feedback, I had a team crisis that required the help of my supervisors. Among other faults of mine, I am a recovering perfectionist and failing as a leader in what felt like a devastating way crushed me. I still stand by some of my decisions, but I also know that I could've and should've done some things differently. While I was sitting in the proverbial "rock bottom," I was invited to apply for a promotion. My supervisor told me I had a choice: I could let this experience of failure define my leadership, or I could learn from failure and continue leading.

Part of maintaining the status quo is also a relational transaction. We don't want to lose relationships by hurting our friends and family. We (meaning I) also don't want to have to make more friends. Sometimes speaking up runs the risk of hurt feelings, and that's a real concern. People who claim to love Jesus shouldn't be running around saying things with no regard for others. However, there is a way in which individualism trumps community in the western context. Speaking out against injustice isn't about my personal feelings and opinions being prioritized over someone else's feelings and opinions—instead, it's about recognizing that our individual feelings and opinions about a situation are secondary in importance to the overall impact on our community and society.

One of the ways we experience this is the phenomenon known as "white tears." This term, often used for comedic effect, is when a white person has their feelings hurt by what they perceive to be racial injustice, especially when a person of color has said or done something that pushes back on white privilege, and those hurt feelings take center stage over the real issue of justice—ergo, white tears. For example, *American Idol* runner-up Bo Bice threatened legal action against a food chain, claiming that an employee referred to him as "that white boy."[4] Bice said he was the victim of racism and talked about feeling humiliated—he literally cried "white tears." Online commentators jumped in and called him out for his tone-deaf statements. I have no doubt Bice's feelings were affected by what happened. But Bice and his supporters never stopped to address the broader, systemic issues of racism that obviously don't affect white people in the same way as they affect people of color. For him and his fans, the focus literally was on his tears.

I can only imagine that is a little bit of what Mordecai experienced with his niece, Queen Esther. When Esther finds out that the Jews are facing annihilation and they need someone to speak up on their behalf, her first response is driven by fear for her own life. I imagine that Mordecai might have thought, "Esther, why worry about dying because the king might not recognize you? *All Jews,* including you, *are going to die!* Get over yourself right now and pull it together!"

INVISIBLE LANDMINES

Power dynamics and cultural norms can also keep us from speaking up. This builds on maintaining the status quo and being aware of hurting other people unnecessarily. It involves issues of gender, race, ethnicity, and culture as well as generational values and workplace dynamics. It gets complicated rather quickly and there's no easy roadmap to guide us.

In certain cultures, elders are respected and revered. The unspoken rule is that you never question, shame, or embarrass an elder in public or directly. In chapter one, I shared a story about when I was physically silenced in a meeting. The context involved workplace dynamics as well as cultural values. The meeting was of all Asian American staff attending a national meeting, and we were gathered because of a crisis involving some of our Asian American senior staff. When I asked questions, I was breaking cultural norms by directly questioning an elder in our community in public. I was also sitting next to someone who was both my elder and my supervisor. The public silencing I experienced was shocking, but it wasn't clearly right or wrong when taking that context into account. Speaking out in those types of situations is extremely complicated because we are juggling hierarchy, timing, gender, and a fluid sense of what specific actions will maintain harmony. However, in any circumstance there are always unspoken rules of engagement. If we never challenge them, we may perpetuate unhealthy patterns and never actually address and resolve conflict.

Navigating power dynamics in any situation requires learning and awareness for all parties. My first job out of college was as a reporter in a newsroom in Green Bay, Wisconsin.

Calling professors by their first names was difficult in college, and then I experienced another level of cultural whiplash when my newspaper bosses, even the editor-in-chief, requested I call them by their first names. In peer-to-peer situations, I would've had no problem speaking up in meetings or arguing a point, but journalism school didn't prepare me to fight for my story or argue for better story placement. I didn't know how to self-promote my story to Roger or Joanne when I was keenly aware that there were reporters more senior than me in the room. I was operating out of a set of unspoken rules that were culturally bound, while other reporters more easily fought to get the top story position. It wasn't personal. It wasn't communal. It was business as usual in a US newsroom.

Another thing college didn't prepare me for was fatigue—specifically justice and race fatigue. People of color often become the default expert on all matters of race and justice in a way that white allies do not. While I do speak and write quite a bit about race, ethnicity, gender, and justice, I also know a thing or two about leadership, mentoring, parenting, marriage, and organizing closets. I enjoy speaking and writing about justice, but I get tired of being the speaker on a panel who is supposed to represent all Asian Americans. There are more than 18.9 million of us in the United States[5] representing twenty-four distinct groups.[6] How can one person possibly capture the diversity of that experience? But that is what I and other people of color are asked to do. We are expected to take something complex and complicated and reduce it to something manageable and easy in order to educate people quickly and efficiently (and we often aren't paid or paid well).

Even in the church there is uncertainty about how we interact with, engage, and welcome people who have a critical edge. In evangelical circles, we like to call people like me *prophetic*—a label I would never give myself; I still cringe a little when someone calls me a prophetic voice. Sometimes that label can be interpreted as a euphemism for troublemaker, annoying, or opinionated. Sometimes it's used sincerely and with respect. I'm not comfortable with the label of prophet because prophets in the Bible don't seem happy and are often lonely and tired. I suppose prophets in the Old Testament could also have suffered from justice fatigue. Regardless, the Old Testament prophets not only recorded history but also remind the modern church of the need for people who say things that need to be said, even when it's uncomfortable, unpopular, and dangerous. The apostle Paul reminds us that there is diversity of purpose and function for the body of Christ even as we are called to unity.

So Christ himself gave the apostles, the prophets, the evangelists, the pastors and teachers, to equip his people for works of service, so that the body of Christ may be built up until we all reach unity in the faith and in the knowledge of the Son of God and become mature, attaining to the whole measure of the fullness of Christ. (Ephesians 4:11-13)

The final reason people may choose not to speak up is due to self-preservation. For some people, speaking up is dangerous. I'm not an evangelical who believes Christians in the United States are being persecuted. However, I do believe that our current sociopolitical circumstances have made it physically dangerous for certain groups of people—black and brown people, immigrants, refugees, and Muslims—to speak out against injustice. When they do, they face real threats to their physical safety.

Even in the face of danger, some of us will still choose to speak up. Why, when all worldly wisdom would suggest staying quiet is the best option, do ordinary people in ordinary circumstances choose to speak up? It happens when we are desperate, clinging to the hope of change. We face our fears and trust Jesus is inviting us to speak up. This moment of truth looks different for everyone, but we can learn a lot from the story in the Bible of the bleeding woman.

NO LONGER AN OPTION

We don't know her name and only know her by her physical affliction. The woman in Mark 5 has had an irregular menstrual flow, incurable for twelve years, which means she was considered ceremoniously unclean and cut off from normal interactions with people for a long time. She spent whatever money she had and continued to suffer, finding no relief despite every effort. She has no family, no patriarch to speak on her behalf. The woman is literally broken and bleeding. In an act of absolute desperation, she simply touches Jesus' cloak in hopes that it could heal her.

According to law, this woman was supposed to announce to the crowd that she was unclean lest anyone touch her and then also become ceremoniously unclean. Instead, she stays silent yet speaks out with her actions, reaching for the edge of Jesus' cloak. Her bleeding stops immediately. Before she can get away from the crowd, Jesus, knowing power has gone out of him, asks his disciples who touched him—which, at face value, is a ridiculous question to ask when a crowd is pressing against him. Everyone and no one had touched him. Jesus waits for an answer, giving the woman a chance to speak up:

> But Jesus kept looking around to see who had done it. Then the woman, knowing what had happened to her, came and fell at his feet and, trembling with fear, told him the whole truth. He said to her, "Daughter, your faith has healed you. Go in peace and be freed from your suffering." (Mark 5:32-34)

The woman doesn't run away, realizes that Jesus is waiting for her, and overcomes her fear to tell her story to Jesus, in no small part because he created space for her to tell her story.

Jesus calls her "daughter," thereby restoring her back into the community. He announces that it was the woman's faith and not his power that healed her. He grants her peace and freedom, not specifically from the actual bleeding but from the suffering she has had to endure from twelve years of isolation. He sends her back into community.

We can find ourselves both in the story of the woman and the story of the witnessing crowd. We are challenged by this example of a woman who had nothing left to lose, who chose to speak up and not run away. We are also in the crowd that witnessed this amazing thing happen. This castaway, with no one to care for her, overcame stigma and cultural norms. She defied the law to seek healing from Jesus in front of a crowd that could've condemned her for her brazen actions. Jesus waited for her to speak up, and now the break in the story is a chance for the community, for us, to speak up.

What will we say after we hear the woman's story? What will we say when Jesus gives us a chance to speak up?

Part 2

HOW TO
SPEAK UP

Chapter 5

IRL (IN REAL LIFE)

*S*peaking up assumes there is an audience, whether it's IRL (In Real Life) or online. In this chapter, we will look at the types of real life, in-the-flesh audiences and some general guidelines to help you speak up. In the next chapter, we will tackle digital spaces where many of us are connecting and perhaps disconnecting.

Your real-life relationships and circles of influence, whether you're single or married, start at home and move outward, with some spaces overlapping each other. Home and friends overlap when you invite friends into your space. Church and work might overlap if you have coworkers who attend worship services with you.

Home is where you make it, and it can be both physical and spiritual. For me, it's both my actual house and also spending time with the people I love, wherever we are. Home is where I hear and can speak my heart language of rice, pajamas, sheet masks, and late night talks. It's also where I am the most vulnerable and most prone to reveal the very best and very worst in me. It's where my family has heard me scream and yell at them, and it's where they have seen me cry and be at the end of myself. Home is also where cultural values often clash, mix, and blend against more layers of differences such as generational, socioeconomic, or religious. A safe and secure home provides us with a place to develop and use our authentic voice to love and bring about change. Home can also become unsafe spaces when relationships are unhealthy or abusive.

Wherever and with whomever we call home, it's where the rubber meets the road. It's where our public and private words come up against how we live every day, and those words are amplified in powerful, face-to-face ways.

UNDERWEAR FAMILY

Your first circle of relationships is with your next of kin, the people who have seen you in your underwear. This group may or may not include a spouse, children, parents, siblings, housemates, college best friends, and childhood friends. These people know you in a way no one else does, and because of that, sometimes they think they know you and you think you know them, even though that may be versions of you and them that are frozen in time, embellished with recent interactions.

For me, this group includes my spouse of almost twenty-five years and three children who are young adults at various stages of frontal lobe development and financial independence. They are the ones who have heard me talk about taking anti-depressants and my therapy sessions and about putting their clothes away for the sake of their future spouses and roommates.

They are also the ones who hear me talk back at the television. I really didn't think it was a problem. Our family has a habit of responding out loud to things we hear whether we're at home or behind the wheel (never at the movie theater, though). However, I stopped when my oldest son, Corban, starting yelling at the news—he was parroting me. This wasn't a cute YouTube video moment where a precocious child provides commentary like a sarcastic adult. It horrified me to see my son repeat things he had heard me say before he was old enough to formulate opinions for himself.

HOLIDAY FAMILY

This is your second circle of relationships. Over the years, we have had different people join us for the holidays, but the key players are always extended family—parents, siblings, and their families and/or significant others, nieces, nephews, cousins, aunties, and uncles. Many people now celebrate Friendsgiving, gathering with friends a few days before the big family dinner. Regardless of the guest list, we must learn to navigate holidays and special occasions when there are things we want to say.

My extended family doesn't really understand what I do vocationally, in part because some of them don't share my faith tradition. Perhaps it's confusing that I spend as much time writing and communicating online as I do in meetings and ministering for my current day job. This lack of understanding keeps me grounded, humble, and sometimes frustrated. But I have never blocked them from what I do publicly on social media. When a relative and I had a few public online exchanges, it made me wonder if I was ready to engage my extended family about racial and socioeconomic injustice, politics, and faith. This relative commented on a few of my posts about racism and justice, and there were several moments when I wondered if I should intervene and do what I usually never do—come to someone else's defense when other commentators push back.

I didn't intervene and instead let social media run its course. I didn't stop other posters from challenging my relative, nor did I come to his defense, primarily because I couldn't and wouldn't defend his opinions or line of questioning.

I also decided not to confront my relative about those social media exchanges or question his opinions at our next extended family gathering. I took into consideration if there would be an opportunity to have a one-on-one conversation as opposed to an open discussion around the dinner table. I took this person's maturity level into account and also how I was related to this person, how they related to the other guests, and how a potentially tense conversation would affect our time together. I also considered whether or not we could come to a healthy, helpful resolution if we talked with others around. I had to examine my motivations—did I want to confront this person because I wanted to be right? Am I in a place to really listen to this person?

After my assessment, I realized that I was feeling too prickly in that moment, and I recognized it wasn't the time to try to prove my case. My heart wasn't ready.

YOUR PEOPLE

This is the next circle of relationships. I've heard this circle of influence referred to as "your tribe." This phrase feels a bit appropriative to me, especially considering that our government nearly obliterated Native American tribes—and now we use the term to describe friendships that positively identify and define us. But I digress.

This group of people is the family you choose, so to speak. They are the ones who use any reason to get together, including sports championships, season finales of television shows, birthdays, major and minor holidays, grief, and celebration. Sometimes different individuals come and go depending on the specifics of the gathering, but I have found that a core group is important. If we don't have this kind of group in our lives, we are looking for it.

In our attempt to find this group, my spouse and I threw legendary-in-our-own-minds parties around the ABC television show *Lost*, which included wearing costumes and serving themed food. People who didn't even enjoy the show wanted to come because they saw our commitment.

Finding a common language and interest is a great way to find friends. We wanted to know people not only in our church but also in our neighborhood. For that reason, I started a book club with my neighbor so I could get to know her and other women nearby. We had been in the neighborhood a few years, and I hadn't been able to find a group of women to call true friends. We read Kathryn Stockett's *The Help* and had many great and sometimes tense conversations about the merits of the book. Speaking up in a group never gets easier, nor does the process of making good friends—but I have learned both are worth the effort.

MEET THE NEIGHBORS

I live in a very white community. According to census data, my village of 20,315 residents is 90 percent white. My family of five helps bring the Asian American population to 5 percent.[1] When we first decided to move to our neighborhood, we knew we weren't moving into a diverse community. But we liked the area because it served as an in-between space for us—in between family in two nearby suburbs, in between families in our church small group, in between starter-homes and McMansions, and in between the working-class suburb I grew up in and the upper-class suburbs where many of our Korean American peers were moving. My spouse and I are both college-educated, and we fit socio-economically. We both grew up in very white suburbs. We thought it would be fine.

It wasn't. We now have a good circle of neighborhood friends, but the first several years were difficult to navigate as we found our bearings as a family. I had to learn to navigate different spheres as a working mom whose office was at home. We had to find a new church after attending a Korean American second-generation church for almost a decade. I had to decide whether I would make or allow my children to walk home unaccompanied and enjoy the relative safety of the community or be the mom who showed up to greet her children at the school playground when the bell rang (I did a mix when I was not traveling). We had to find new friends, and our kids had to find new friends. I thought being in my thirties meant finally being comfortable in my own skin, but I didn't know what that meant until I was desperate for connection. I found myself resorting to Midwest nice while trying to make new friends. It was easier and less threatening to talk about how fun the Pilgrim Celebration was rather than ask out loud if anyone else thought having an adult man dressed in a generic Native American costume and speaking stilted English like Tonto was the least bit offensive. Have you ever felt like you weren't sure how much to bring of your real personality, personal opinions, and interests to any conversation for fear that you would offend someone, step on some toes, say something too divisive, and miss out on an opportunity for a friend? No? Me neither.

The road to loving your neighbor felt that much longer and more difficult because I had not factored in the time and effort it would take to meet and get to know my new non-Asian American neighbors and church goers.

Raising Her Voice

I have to say something, Brenda thought as she considered her concerns about the Pilgrim Celebration at her son's school—the same school and celebration my children had attended years before.[a] Brenda was concerned about her son participating in what she felt was an offensive tradition in which students, dressed as pilgrims, and their parents, dressed in generic Native American costumes, play games against each other.

As Brenda spoke with me about it, she said, "I had to say something. It's what I had to do." As an advocate who coordinates programs to end homelessness, Brenda is used to speaking up, although her usual coping mechanism is to avoid difficult situations such as questioning a dearly held school tradition.

Brenda did some research about the celebration before approaching the school principal. She put together a list of talking points as well as questions. Why include questions?

"Seek first to understand, then to be understood. I know it sounds like the Bible, but it's not. It's Stephen Covey," she answered, laughing. She also got other people's opinions, talking to her sister, a veteran teacher, about the event. Brenda decided that she was going to approach the situation as a parent who was concerned about what her child was going to learn.

"Don't teach the wrong history. [The celebration is] marginalizing the culture of people who look different. This is about school culture, values, and diversity," she said. "My biggest fear about raising a child in this community is I'm raising an entitled white boy."

Brenda asked for a meeting with the school principal. She went in prepared with a copy of photographs from the previous year's celebration and a list of talking points, hoping to communicate shared values and a common vision for a value of inclusion.

The meeting didn't bring immediate success. The principal responded with a cordial email acknowledging Brenda's concerns and suggested that if she was still concerned with the celebration, she and her child didn't have to participate. She could've given up at that point, but she decided to keep going and wrote an email to the district superintendent, with no expectations of a response.

One day later she received an email from the superintendent. It said that he had had a conversation with the American Indian Center of Chicago, and that changes were being made to the event and the curriculum. Five days after that, the second grade parents were notified that the Pilgrim Celebration would no longer include a reenactment of parents playing the role of Native Americans but instead would include a Native American speaker presenting on native history, music, and traditional dress, as well as the life of Pilgrim and Wampanoag children.

Speaking up isn't always the easiest or most expedient thing. And even though Brenda was concerned about how much time and energy speaking up might require, she did it anyway.

"I had to do something. This [meeting with the principal and writing emails], I can do," she said. "If everyone does what they can do, we will all be better off."

[a]*From personal interview with the author, October 2, 2017.*

CHURCH AND STEEPLE, LOVING THE PEOPLE

If you have a church community you can refer to as a second family, consider yourself blessed—and I don't mean "blessed" in a throwing shade at you sort of way. You're fortunate to have found a place to worship, ask questions about faith, bring friends who are in different places in their faith journey, and celebrate and grieve all the things we go through in the course of a lifetime.

In the decade prior to moving to our current home, we attended a pan-Asian American church where we knew what a church potluck would look and taste like (enough food for people to bring home leftovers), how long the musical portion of worship would last (sometimes thirty minutes for the first set), and how we would sing and clap to each song (lots of repetition and clap on beats two and four). We knew that at every house we visited, we would take off our shoes, bring something to eat to share with everyone else, and bring enough to leave with our hosts or for everyone to take home leftovers (it seemed as if we believed in re-enacting the feeding of the five thousand for every small group meeting). We knew what it meant to grieve with one another; Koreans and Korean Americans use a type of ashes and sackcloth with white ribbons to indicate mourning, and there's a formality and depth to the public expression of grief. However, even there, I often had moments of dissonance where, as a woman in vocational ministry, I worried if I was asking too many questions about ethnic identity and women in leadership.

When we moved, we began attending a local community church where our children could grow up with school class-mates and we would interact with people we might run into at the grocery store. It was a huge shift from being at a Korean American church to a white church. We didn't know the rules of engagement, and we didn't know or understand some of the traditions. When you choose to wrestle with questions of privilege, identity, and justice, and you wonder if and when you should use your voice, you may experience some dis-comfort, confusion, and disappointment, no matter where you go to church.

Our family had a chance to learn and function within a culturally white church. One difference from our previous church was moving from a more fluid time orientation—where the beginning and end of service were flexible if additional prayer or musical response was needed—to a linear time orientation in which service started exactly at 10:30 a.m., there were fifteen minutes of music at the start of service, and the whole thing always ended before noon.

I didn't know how at home I had felt at our former church until we left it for another body of believers. My desire to feel at home conflicted with some of the values and cultural norms presented at our new church that are not intended to leave people feeling on the outside. I'm a columnist for our denomination's bimonthly magazine, and that has been awkward. My writing voice is conversational and vulnerable, but I don't know if I've figured out how to speak up about being a Korean American woman attending a white church. When I'm writing a column and deciding on how to raise my voice, I go through a lengthy series of questions in my heart and mind:

- Can I love my neighbors, the white sisters and brothers I sit with in the pews, even as I wrestle through my confusion and frustration with the church's relative silence and delay in addressing systemic racism and injustice?

- Can they love me?

- How much speaking up in this context is too much, when the universal response to wanting change seems to be that change is difficult and takes time?

- How can I make sure people at my church understand that my concerns and questions are not a critique of individuals but instead are questioning the systems we choose to maintain?

I haven't figured out all the answers yet, but one thing I'm sure about is that speaking up in a community for the community isn't something you can opt out of. Eventually we all have to recognize that now is always the time to speak up against injustice, even when people respond by stopping you in the stairwell and apologizing.

My main exchanges with a man named Daniel at church were brief conversations about church and vague references to my column. But recently, we exchanged a series of text messages that went from good to horrible within about five messages. It started when I shared a link with him about systemic racism, but because I didn't include anything about why I was sharing the particular story, Daniel assumed I was accusing him of the same racist behaviors described in the article. He was angry and hurt that I would lump him in with racists. Days later, he stopped me in the stairwell at church to talk. Daniel had read one of my columns about white fragility[2]—the tendency of white people to get defensive at the first sign of racial stress. He had recognized himself in my column and his text exchanges with me. It was a holy moment of apology and forgiveness.

THE DAILY GRIND

For those of us fortunate enough to have jobs, we also need to consider the office and work colleagues as another sphere of relationships and influence. Even if you don't have a physical office, you still interact with colleagues, bosses, and perhaps subordinates.

Corporate culture dynamics run the gamut, but there are a few things that apply to most situations that you should consider when speaking up in meetings or speaking out against workplace injustice.

- The issue of power: Are you the boss or the employee in the situation? How does your position of power affect how your message will be received, interpreted, or applied? How might other people be affected when you speaking up? What safeguards are in place for whistle-blowers? Read about whistleblower protection programs enforced through the Occupational Safety and Health Administration (OSHA) under the United States Department of Labor at www.whistleblowers.gov.

- The issue of policy: Is the issue you want to address a relational one, where a conversation is the best route? Or does the issue require you to consider more formal processes through a human resources representative?

- The issue of commitment: How committed are you? Speaking up requires you to consider how to be faithful to the work. Is it worth it to say something? Will it affect your ability to accomplish your daily tasks?

- The issue of consequences: Is there a possible negative impact of staying silent? What are the consequences of speaking up?

DIFFERENT BUT SAME

Now that you've considered some of the different spheres in which you can use your voice, it's time to think about what you need to consider as you speak up. Each sphere of influence has its unique opportunities and challenges, but there are some universal things to do before you speak up, while you speak up, and after you speak up.

Before you speak up:

- Pray. Make sure you know your motivation for speaking up, because it shouldn't be about merely creating or causing conflict. Your deeper motivation should actually be about applying the gospel message to the situation. When we speak up because a situation is "wrong" or "not right," it should be grounded in our faith and understanding of what this world is meant to look, feel, and be like according to the Word. Prayer should be our starting point.

- Do your research. Know your facts. You don't want to speak up against or for something you know little about. This isn't about emotions or feelings, though they will come up and need to be expressed. This is about speaking up against an injustice such as racism, or speaking up for something positive and beneficial such as availability and access to healthcare.

- Figure out what your position is in the situation. Why do *you* care? You may not always be directly affected, negatively or positively, as you increase awareness around a particular issue. Know why you are speaking up.

- Prepare your talking points, whether you are communicating via email or face-to-face. How will you communicate respect to people who hold differing opinions than you while you're articulating your concerns?

- Imagine worst-case scenarios. Can you deal with a negative end result? Even if you think nothing will change, do you still want to say or do something?

- Imagine best-case scenarios. What is the best outcome? Can you settle for small changes? If you could see only one thing change, what would it be?

While you speak up:

- Pray. The person you talk with or send an email to may be caught completely off-guard while you've had time to mentally prepare. Pray for the interaction to reflect mutual respect and honor the *imago Dei* in others.

- Breathe. Emotions can run high, even when we are convinced saying or doing something is right and just and even when our comments are positive and affirming. You may need to slow down (or speed up!) the conversation to deal with emotions. Emotions should help us keep in tune with what's going on internally in our hearts and minds and connect that to our bodies.

- Ask questions. You are ready to speak up, but if we are genuinely interested in influencing others, raising awareness, and changing the hearts and minds of other people, we need to listen and ask questions. We need to understand how our message is being received and how people are hearing our voices. Ask them about their concerns, thoughts, and hopes.

- Know your power. I need to check how I'm using my authority or my advantage as a fast thinker, especially when I'm speaking up in a family context. When I'm speaking up in a work context, I need to be aware that, as a woman of color in senior leadership, my words carry a great deal of weight in a room—as does my silence.

After you speak up:

- Pray. Speaking up is a matter of stewarding our power and accepting God's invitation to engage certain matters. It's spiritual work that still brings me to my knees.

- Follow up. Speaking up isn't always a one-time comment in a meeting or sharing an opinion at the dinner table. Oftentimes, we are in ongoing relationships with the people we've challenged. And we need to remember that speaking up isn't just so we can hear our own voices— it's about our willingness to be held accountable to the values or issues we are most passionate about. It's a way we hope to bring about change and understanding. Did the person who heard us really hear us? Are there changes afoot?

- Start all over again.

When Speaking Up Causes Conflict

Use both digital and IRL opportunities to engage and build trust. Don't just be a supplier of information and opinions. Engage with what your neighbors are posting and saying. We all want points of personal connection and mutual interest.

Not everyone is going to like what you have to say. Remember, speaking up isn't about presenting an easily accepted message. It's about addressing injustice—big and small.

Don't assign intent to someone's words, posts, or actions. I can't read minds—just ask my spouse and family—and you can't read minds either. We can only take a good look at our personal reactions and intentions and then figure out why we feel the way we do and why we responded the way we did.

Don't assume a person's tone, whether you are in a digital space or IRL. Ask clarifying questions so the person can tell more of their story.

I choose to speak up, over and over again, even when it's awkward because awkwardness is easier to overcome than allowing injustice to continue.

When you want to speak with someone you know IRL and can talk with them in person, always choose face-to-face interactions (or at least by phone) when possible.

Chapter 6

WHEN YOU POST IT

EVERYONE AND NO ONE WILL CARE

f you can't say anything nice, don't say anything at all . . . unless it's on social media. On social media, it seems you can say whatever you want whenever you want to.

The public square continues to change at a rapid pace. Using your voice in the virtual world can take the form of blogs, status updates, tweets, memes, videos, and images that seem to disappear but actually are archived for digital eternity. Speaking up in the digital space was previously limited to email, which challenged us to consider the power of face-to-face interactions and compare what was lost and gained by moving communication into a virtual space. The rise of email usage affected the way, speed, and nature of how we communicate. When email was limited to only words, it left room for interpretation of tone and meaning and sometimes led to misunderstanding and possible conflict.

The upside of email is that it broadened our reach with the ability to communicate the same message to a larger audience. And with the addition of images and graphics, an element of creativity and visual interest has been added to email that helps communicate messages that words alone could not convey.

Now there are many social media platforms vying for our attention and mastery. We can spend so much time reading or producing content that we don't realize how social media can be useful or even necessary in speaking out, communicating our message, and affecting change.

It's easy to get sucked into social media. We may think that our digital voice is either meaningless (because it's just a cat meme) or extremely powerful (because it's a quote about immigration reform). The truth is that it's somewhere in between. Because of this ambiguity, it's often the easiest space to project a false self, using a false voice. We may believe that it's easiest to say whatever we want when in a digital space, with little consequence.

RULES OF ENGAGEMENT

For those of us who cut our social media teeth on Facebook, the world has changed. We are now able to share everything about ourselves and our mundane lives whenever and wherever we want via Twitter, Instagram, or Snapchat. We can share music playlists on Spotify and crowdsource book recommendations on Goodreads. Depending on the number of people and organizations you follow, keeping up with your feed takes a bit of effort, discipline, and self-restraint.

Even if you think you aren't speaking up about anything in particular when you post family photos or cat memes, you are. Nothing we do or say is without meaning and a deeper message. Why did I post that amazing photo of my sons dressed up for the school dance? I wanted my extended family and friends (all 2,000-plus of them) to see how handsome my sons look in their suits. That's innocent enough. But why didn't I just send the photo via email to my parents? Do the 2,000-plus people on my social media accounts—people I don't usually interact with on a personal, face-to-face basis—actually need to see the photo? My sons shared the same photo, with captions that express their close friendship as siblings. Still innocent? Sort of. But there was definitely an intent to communicate a certain message with our posts. Whenever we post something on social media, it's never *just* a post. This isn't a judgment on what you post—it's a word of caution.

In the digital space, there is a saying: "If you wouldn't say something to a person face-to-face, don't put it in a text." Because of the virtual nature of social media, it can be easy to lose sight of the people on the receiving end of the message. We can't hear their voices and, in many cases, we may not even have a face or real name, just a Twitter handle or image. My Facebook avatar until recently was an upside-down flag, which I started using in December 2014. An upside-down flag connotes distress, and in the fall of 2014, several publicized incidents of police violence against black men and women caused me to rethink a lot of my beliefs, including what my smiling photo communicated. I wrote about the decision to change my avatar in a blog,[1] and two years later I was still getting asked publicly and privately about the story behind my avatar. People who I initially met on social media but who I now call friends adopted the same avatar after reading my blog.

The old adage is true: you attract more bees with honey, so when someone asks with honest curiosity about my upside-down flag avatar, I respond politely and invite them into a conversation. I patiently field questions about my silent protest, but on occasion I have been accused of being un-American, an ignorant immigrant, and other words my editor won't allow. Those negative comments usually aren't actual inquiries, and depending on how my prayer life is that day, I try to choose not to engage. Instead, I choose to stop, take a breath, and remember the person on the other side of the IP address is created in God's image, whether or not I want to treat them that way. In a virtual world where I want my words and actions to reflect Jesus, my response should be one that is respectful, gracious, and kind. Sometimes, my tendency toward a snarky comment and sarcasm gets the best of me. Other times, Jesus and hope mixed with a touch of snark wins.

How will I interact with someone, regardless of their avatar or social media handle, especially if that person disagrees strongly with my opinions or, even worse, begins to attack me personally? How will any of us respond when our words, either flippantly posted or thrown out into the ether with caution, are met with anger and personal attack? We must not confuse using courage to speak up with responding in cowardice by lashing out because the medium affords us a degree of anonymity.

TRUE SELF/FALSE SELF

Before Facebook, there was Webkinz, toy stuffed animals that carried social cachet among the elementary school set. Webkinz made their debut in the spring of 1999, but it wasn't until a few years later, when my children were ages nine, five, and three, that the obsession hit home. They were too young to understand the power of supply and demand, but they responded just like the economists expected. Each stuffed animal came with a code you entered online to gain access to a digital pet shop where your toy "came to life" on the screen. You would have to take good care of the pet in order to gain digital currency and special bonuses and keep your digital pet alive and living in luxury. The power wasn't just in snagging the rare stuffed animal; it was also about creating a little kingdom for your pet. Now, more than ten years later, I have a laundry hamper full of Webkinz, once some of their most prized possessions. It's a physical reminder of the time and birthday money spent on pet cities of Babel that now lie in digital dust.

Children are not the only ones drawn into the virtual world. Social media and the internet have been primarily places for adults, and the interaction can be addicting. Researchers are finding that a decade of smartphone usage changes us and has the potential to increase anxiety, raise blood pressure, and negatively affect our ability to focus.[2] Our brains respond to rewards (every time I hit a word count milestone on this manuscript, I gave myself a lovely piece of dark chocolate), even when it isn't a physical pat on the back. A virtual stroking of the ego is a strong drug.[3]

The line between our true self and false self, which is difficult enough to walk in the real world, is made even more complex on social media and its different platforms with different audiences. Social media can provide an easy trap for thinking you're a bigger deal than you actually are. I speak from experience.

Blogging started out as a professional obligation more than ten years ago after I coauthored a book for InterVarsity Press titled *More Than Serving Tea*. The editor, Al Hsu, told my coauthors and me that a well-known theologian had mentioned the book on his blog. Al recommended that we comment on the blog to start a dialogue and perhaps generate more interest in what was considered a niche book. He also suggested that we should consider blogging under the name of the book. About a year into writing for the *More Than Serving Tea* blog, we realized I was the only one still blogging. I took over the blog, moved it, and eventually renamed and rebranded it, connecting it to Facebook, Twitter, and Instagram.

Between 2013 and 2015, I had the run of a lifetime in my professional world. Due to a series of successful paid speaking engagements, I developed an overly heightened sense of self-importance while simultaneously wrestling with imposter syndrome. I was speaking at the same events as established Christian speakers and authors such as Jen Hatmaker, Bob Goff, Lauren Winner, Rachel Held Evans, and Shauna Niequist. I knew I wasn't a bad speaker, and I would remind myself that no one knew who I was, so the bar for evaluating my performance was low for me; it would be easier to exceed expectations. Could I be a good speaker? Could I be a great speaker?

Do you see where this was going and why it became a problem? Too many "I" statements meant too much time sitting in that false self. But the bigger stages and bigger names were a drug.

The invitations to speak publicly were also an invitation from God to speak the truths and questions in my heart and to invite a larger audience to speak those same truths and ask God those same questions: "Is it okay to have ambitions and to be ambitious? What does stewarding my gifts for the kingdom look like? What does it look like to live fully into God's gifts and invitations when all the examples are white men and women? Does God's 'kingdom come and will be done on earth as it is in heaven' include a Korean American married mom of three?"

Fortunately, I return home after speaking engagements. Nothing equalizes the ego quite as much as a family and friends who are supportive but not overly impressed with me.

A friend gave me a framed print that reads, "I am kind of a big deal on my blog." It hangs just to my left when I'm sitting at my desk, and I look at it when I get up at the end of a writing session. It's a loving, whimsical reminder to deflate my head so that it will fit through the door when I leave. Across from my desk is small but growing collection of crosses and spiritual art to remind me that I write at the invitation and call of Jesus.

So, you're not a public speaker and can't relate? Well, if you're on social media, you consciously or subconsciously know the nudging of the ego and the rush of public approval. Researchers are learning we get a rush of dopamine, "a neurochemical known as the 'reward molecule' that's released after certain human actions or behaviors, such as exercising, or setting and achieving a goal."[4] Those "likes" on a post are like a drug that makes you feel good about yourself.

The opposite can happen when you post something and don't get the response you hoped for or expected. I'm known to jump into online conversations about topics I am passionate about, and a recent exchange with a colleague provided the opportunity to talk on the phone about what had happened online. Brad posted something on our organization's Facebook page, and my comment offered an alternative to what Brad was suggesting. Brad eventually took down his post, removing evidence of the thread that had included several other comments. When I pressed him about his decision to remove the post, he finally said that he was upset when he saw that my comment had gotten more "likes" than his initial post. He isn't alone in his feelings. When we post things on social media, we are hoping for positive feedback. When we don't get that approval, our natural tendency is to retreat. But it's important to remember that engagement on social media isn't about being liked. It's another way of raising our voice to speak truth.

We're wired to desire connection and relationship. When God created humans, it was male *and* female, not just male alone. The creation account explains that it wasn't good for the one to exist without the other. Even in all of creation, there is a synergy and connection—the birds need the air, the fish need the water. We need each other.

Our desire to connect is not limited to physical space and connection, and that's the challenge of speaking out in any situation. The chance you will be misinterpreted remains whether you are in a virtual interaction or face-to-face.

When I share with my spouse the details of a problem I'm facing, I'm not looking for possible solutions. I'm communicating my anxiety and concerns in hopes of receiving empathy, maybe a hug or a knowing look of understanding, and a listening ear. However, when you aren't face-to-face, you don't have physical social cues—facial expressions, audible sighs, or body language. It's true that we don't always perfectly read social cues when we're face-to-face. Whenever we speak our minds, there is plenty of room for misunderstanding. But in the virtual world, communication is faster and broader. Our limitations are exacerbated in many ways when we're online. If speaking off the top of your head isn't your forte, you might want to be cautious about joining comment threads because conversations and exchanges happen at lightning speed. If you choose to jump in (and it's always a choice), the same rules of engagement of real-life interactions also hold in virtual spaces. Be willing to ask for clarification and to be offended and be the offender. Be ready to listen, to assume incorrectly, to be called out, to admit to making a mistake, and to ask for or extend forgiveness. After all, you and the people you're interacting with are only human.

BUILD COMMUNITY AND CULTURE

If you're still willing to engage in the virtual space, the opportunity to learn and connect is great. I've been able to connect digitally with people across the globe living very different lives in different contexts than mine. Social media gives us access not only to news but also to stories from people who love Jesus and want their lives to be an active reflection of love given and received. The challenge is learning to speak this new language while avoiding what happened at the tower of Babel, where people with a common language didn't use that ability to communicate for the common good but instead wanted fame and to create an insular society:

> Then they said, "Come, let us build ourselves a city, with a tower that reaches to the heavens, so that we may make a name for ourselves; otherwise we will be scattered over the face of the whole earth." (Genesis 11:4)

Social media isn't the enemy. It's a tool. But we're our own worst enemies with a natural tendency toward self-preservation, which plays out in the digital space. Remember the story of Esther? She is presented with an opportunity to speak up for the Jewish people—her people—when they're in danger. Why are the Jews going to be annihilated? Because Mordecai refused to kneel down and pay honor to Haman at the king's gate. Think about that. One man refuses to bow down, and the other man's ego and his desire for self-preservation sets off a chain of events that ends with a legal order for genocide.

Actions and words are powerful and can affect change both online and IRL for good or evil. The best and worst example of this is the current state of politics in the United States. Perhaps history books will tell a different story hundreds of years from now, but right now it feels like a hot mess that has spilled into the church. Issues that we have ignored for too long are coming to the forefront. Many faithful evangelical

voters supported Donald Trump, citing his promises to nom-
inate a favorable conservative Supreme Court justice and end
the legal right to abortion. But many other evangelicals are
struggling with the idea that 81 percent of self-identified
white/born-again/evangelical Christians and white Catholics
said they voted for Trump while just 16 percent report they
voted for Hillary Clinton.[5]

Taking that statistic into consideration, along with the
broader narrative of disenfranchised, working-class white
voters, forced the church into a conversation about race. Many
evangelicals, both white and people of color, are asking whether
or not it's worth maintaining the evangelical label for various
reasons. Many of my friends of color and I spent the days
following Trump's win in varying degrees of anger and disbelief.
And while we were not surprised that white evangelicals voted
for Trump, there was something unnerving about knowing
that so many self-identified white Christians, our neighbors
in the pews, had voted for a man whose marital history alone
would have disqualified a more experienced politician of color.
If the election truly was a reflection of a large segment of the
white Christian population wanting to maintain their way of
life, what does that mean for the rest of us?

Many people argue that the best thing we can do now is
just pray for the president and stop being so divisive (at least,
that's what I've been told). To that, I say yes and no. Yes, I
pray for the president and for the world because the things
the president says and does have an impact beyond my personal
well-being and (dis)comfort. However, I don't consider it
divisive to point out the problems as a way to work toward

finding solutions. We can trust in God and still question what is happening around us. We can live out our beliefs even if the ultimate outcome isn't changed for the better.

Mordecai understood that trusting in God doesn't excuse us from speaking up when given an opportunity to name injustice and fight for justice. He admonishes Esther:

> Do not think that because you are in the king's house you alone of all the Jews will escape. For if you remain silent at this time, relief and deliverance for the Jews will arise from another place, but you and your father's family will perish. And who knows but that you have come to your royal position for such a time as this? (Esther 4:13-14)

There is an opportunity for people to talk about systemic injustice in way that can forge new understanding and bring healing individually and systemically, especially on social media where we are able to reach more people in order to educate, learn, and mobilize. Whether or not you personally have chosen to participate in a protest or rally, we can learn from the way organizers build an online presence, spread the word about an action, and generate a sense of community.

On January 27, 2017, Trump signed Executive Order 13769 titled "Protecting the Nation from Foreign Terrorist Entry into the United States." The next morning, Iraqi refugees were detained at John F. Kennedy International Airport in New York, prompting a rally on their behalf. The protest effectively shut down the international terminal and drew international attention. The rally had been publicized and organized primarily via social media, informing people all over the country. People in other cities joined the movement. I read about the plans for Chicago on Facebook. In a rapid flurry of messages within a thirty-minute span on Facebook Messenger, friends let me know that they were going to the rally in Chicago and invited me along. My friend Cortni—my favorite yoga instructor—and I drove together to O'Hare International Airport. During the drive, I learned more about her journey of faith and racial identity as a white woman, something I had not previously had the opportunity to do.

At the airport, I used Facebook's live video streaming to keep people who couldn't attend informed about what was happening. There were a few tables set up in an alcove where lawyers were volunteering their services to people who were being deported. There were moments of silence and sometimes confusion when lawyers and other volunteers updated the crowd. We erupted into cheers and clapping when a family that was being detained was allowed to leave the airport. We shared knowing glances and supportive comments as we chanted. Believe it or not, it felt a little like church.

Social media has become an important part of the protest movements of today. It's a tool that can be used with careful thought in moderation in order to build community as well as to create virtual gathering spaces that can then translate into real life. Remember my story about Webkinz? Well, my children are now twenty-two, eighteen, and sixteen years old, and the two teenagers are gamers who have outgrown their virtual pets and moved onto different roleplaying games with clans and communities. I don't have to understand the games they play, though I've tried, to understand the importance of knowing there is the potential online for so much more than playing games. When people who aren't afraid to speak up for justice are in digital spaces, they are empowered to build each other up rather than tear each other down.

THE RISK

The digital space can be risky and dangerous. My overall strategy with social media began from the role of parent. I intentionally chose to be an early adopter and learn about new, popular platforms before my children were on them, and I continue to learn what I have been telling my children: what gets posted on social media is forever. Even if you delete something, you may not get to it before it makes an impact you can't erase.

Over the past decade, I've been involved in several public, online controversies that involved calling out white Christians on their racism. It usually went something like this: a white Christian posts or says something racist or racially insensitive. Various Asian American Christians and I see or hear it and contact each other to make sure we saw or heard what we thought we saw or heard and to confirm with each other that we aren't crazy for being upset and disappointed in someone we consider to be a fellow believer. We start rather haphazardly sharing the offense publicly because it happened publicly on social media, in or through a publication, or at a national conference. At some point, a smaller group of people organize a more cohesive, pointed response with a plan to further amplify our concerns through key bloggers, theologians, and Christian leaders. They request to talk publicly or privately with the offenders and outline specific requests for follow-up from the offenders. You can Google the following keywords for details on these specific events: Rickshaw Rally, Deadly Viper, Rick Warren Asian American, and Exponential offensive Asian American.

Each controversy was a boot camp in digital organizing, advocacy, and speaking up. There also were private offline interactions as well as public exchanges that resulted in public criticism but also led to some changes. Ultimately those experiences taught me that speaking up is a matter of faithfulness and discernment, and I would re-engage in each of those situations again. I probably will. But before I do, I always ask myself some questions.

Why do it?

Engaging in online exchanges, particularly the larger-scale, organized online actions I've been a part of, is never about creating conflict for conflict's sake. It's always about the truth of the gospel and how it's being incorrectly communicated through stereotypes or through dangerous policies and practices. This isn't about forcing the church to be politically correct or about an individual speaking their mind. It's about how the church and its leaders and members bear false witness in their public leadership. It's about inviting other sisters and brothers to be a church that more accurately reflects the beauty and diversity of the church.[6]

Go alone or with friends?

When responding online to racist behavior or comments, I usually do an initial solo post or two because (1) I want to see if others in my network are seeing/hearing/experiencing the same offense and (2) that invites accountability on my part. Moving forward always involves asking others to join with me, whether it's to speak up online, brainstorm to see what relational connections others may have to the offender, or strategize and pray about next steps. In every one of the online battles I've been a part of, I've leaned heavily on the support and prayers of others because speaking up to power is challenging and humbling. It requires you to consider everyone watching as well as the people directly involved. It also can be extremely lonely, even with multiple people involved.

What about Matthew 18:15?

> If your brother or sister sins, go and point out their fault, just between the two of you. If they listen to you, you have won them over. (Matthew 18:15)

This passage addresses personal offenses. A brother (and in 95 percent of the cases, it's a brother) or sister has sinned publicly. Your neighbor says something offensive while you're chatting at school pick-up. Your aunt says something offensive to you at Thanksgiving while you're washing dishes. Your friend sends you an angry text. All of those are Matthew 18:15 situations. But someone posting a racially offensive image on Facebook when they happen to be the pastor of a megachurch? How would you go and point out their fault in private? You can't. Depending on your networks, you may eventually be able to connect privately with the public figure, but it's difficult for conversations with public figures to stay in private spaces.

What is the end game?

Speaking up, especially to power, for the sake of speaking up can become a dangerous and destructive pattern. Raising your voice is not about creating disruption for disruption's sake. It's always about disrupting something in order to bring about change, something new that better reflects the hope and fullness of the gospel and the kingdom of God here on earth as it is in heaven.

In order to do that, consider what specific changes and action steps you would like to see. This is one thing I didn't do or consider when first starting down this road. I was a bull in a china shop. But then I began to see how the invitation from God wasn't to simply break things but to envision and invite others to rebuild or make a new thing. Asking for a public apology is one thing. Praying and discerning with others in the fight for clear, actionable next steps is actually more difficult that the first Facebook post or tweet posted in anger. We live out the gospel when we reconcile and move forward together.

Do virtual sticks and stones hurt?

Yes. They do. I don't believe Christians who learn to raise their voice should develop a thick skin. Our emotions don't define us. Emotions also should not be ignored. They are the connection between our mind, heart, and body. Sadness or anger also trigger physical reactions that can remind us there's something going on that is deeper than what is on the surface.

In a meeting with my supervisor, I shared the hurt and pain I felt when being told by several other colleagues that I was abrasive and unapproachable. What I didn't expect was to start crying. I had been thinking about these comments for weeks and never physically felt anything. But when I actually spoke the words out loud, the deep betrayal and loneliness in my soul finally had a chance to escape.

When sticks and stones are thrown at you on social media—and they will be if you choose to engage—don't respond until you take a break, breathe, seek the counsel of others, and pray. This is when knowing why you spoke out in the first place is critical.

Is it worth it? Does change really happen?

Yes and yes. Sometimes change is slow, but it can happen, even in virtual spaces. One of those spaces is the Be the Bridge to Racial Unity Facebook group,[7] the online space of Be the Bridge,[8] a community and provider of training resources and curricula to inspire, build, and equip racial bridge builders in the church, founded by Tasha Morrison.

The Facebook group has more than 15,000 members who are asked to spend the first three months in a discipline of active listening—no posting or commenting. The online code of conduct states:

> This does not mean you join the group, check out for three months, then come back and start posting and commenting. During your initial three months, we expect you

to spend time in the group. Read. Watch. Learn. Feel. Examine yourself. Wrestle with God. Become familiar with our terminology and protocols. Active listening is a foundational bridge-building skill. We realize that some of you join our group with years or even decades of racial reconciliation experience. We have much we can learn from you, but we still require you to enter into this discipline. Anyone who abuses this rule will be removed from the group.

Another online rule is that Sundays are a day of rest when only prayers, music, poetry, or artwork are allowed on a single thread. This clear onramp process, along with a committed group of moderators and long-time members, has created an online environment that welcomes people where they are in their personal racial or ethnic identity journey and encourages everyone to listen, learn, and engage.

Heated discussions inevitably happen, and there is no shortage of topics from which these can stem, but week after week participants post honest questions and receive honest answers from other Christians genuinely interested in having the difficult conversations around race that Morrison rightfully says should be led by the church.

That space has served as a reminder to me that speaking up is never about creating conflict or being disruptive just to shake things up and leave a mess. Speaking up is always about the gospel—speaking and painting a picture of truth, wholeness, and hope. What a powerful tool in social media we have at our disposal to communicate the gospel and learn about the gospel with others around the world!

Learn from My Mistakes

Here's my advice on best practices for raising your voice in the digital world.

Dos:

- Do comment on your online friends' posts about what you find interesting, challenging, or helpful about their post.
- Do check your privacy settings in all of your social media accounts and decide what you want public and what you want shared only with friends.
- Do share articles, blogs, images, and news articles and describe how you are learning or being challenged. Explain to your online community why you share what you share.
- Do block and report people who are abusive and threatening.
- Do check to see if your employer has a social media policy.
- Do remember that the internet is forever. Things you share only with friends can be captured and shared with the world before you get around to deleting a post you regret.
- Do ask for permission if you want to post photographs or stories that involve other people, especially other people's children.
- Do take social media breaks.
- Do say goodnight to the screen at least an hour before bedtime.

Don'ts:

- Don't post anything on social media you wouldn't want your spouse, parents, children, pastor, or best friend to see.
- Don't post anything you wouldn't want to see in the *New York Times* or trending on Twitter.
- Don't post something if you're unwilling to engage in an online dialogue with people you disagree with.
- Don't post unless you're willing to play mediator between friends on your page who disagree, and decide how you're going to moderate threads and handle discourse.

- Don't forget you're the master of your social media space. You can decide the boundaries.
- Don't assume what you're posting on your own time won't get you in trouble with your employer.
- Don't gossip or slander by telling a story, even if you change the names. Just because you're doing it virtually doesn't change the fact that it's gossip.
- Don't feed the trolls.
- Don't let your children keep their electronic devices in their rooms overnight. It's probably a good rule for adults too (I should probably just get an old-fashioned alarm clock).

Chapter 7

EVERYONE HAS A PART

W hen it comes to using our voices to affect change, it's important to know we all play different parts in the issues we care about. That is the beauty of the kingdom of God. We can be unified in mission while maintaining our uniqueness and diversity. Paul uses the physical body as an example of how, by design, we are each different and unique but can work together.

> Just as a body, though one, has many parts, but all its many parts form one body, so it is with Christ. For we were all baptized by one Spirit so as to form one body— whether Jews or Gentiles, slave or free—and we were all given the one Spirit to drink. Even so the body is not made up of one part but of many.
>
> Now if the foot should say, "Because I am not a hand, I do not belong to the body," it would not for that reason stop being part of the body. And if the ear should say, "Because I am not an eye, I do not belong to the body," it would not for that reason stop being part of the body. If

the whole body were an eye, where would the sense of hearing be? If the whole body were an ear, where would the sense of smell be? But in fact God has placed the parts in the body, every one of them, just as he wanted them to be. If they were all one part, where would the body be? As it is, there are many parts, but one body. . . . If one part suffers, every part suffers with it; if one part is honored, every part rejoices with it. (1 Corinthians 12:12-20, 26)

John writes in Revelation how, even in a vision of the future, God sees individuals, recognizes differences, and remains embodied in them as they are standing, wearing, holding, and using their voices to cry out.

After this I looked, and there before me was a great multitude that no one could count, from every nation, tribe, people and language, standing before the throne and before the Lamb. They were wearing white robes and were holding palm branches in their hands. And they cried out in a loud voice:

> "Salvation belongs to our God,
> who sits on the throne,
> and to the Lamb." (Revelation 7:9-10)

FIND YOUR VOICE IN YOUR HEART

There is so much in this world that grabs our attention and hearts. We could be marching in protest or support of something every single day. However, not everyone is called or gifted to be a community organizer. Not everyone has the ability and means to take a few days off to drive to Washington,

DC, like Bethany, Tina, and I did in January 2017. And not everyone who cares deeply about women around the world is compelled or able to take to the streets. Some of us are the feet, or hands, or eyes, or ears, and thankfully we all are moved by our hearts and souls to figure out what role we will play.

The things that make us move out of our hearts and souls to express and embody our values will be different. As a person who wears her emotions on her sleeve and whose emotions break for so many things, I've learned that we can't speak out about all of the things all of the time with equal energy. You will need to know which race you want to run and how to, or if you want to, stay in your lane.

On social media, you can see this pulling and tugging happen in real time. Posting about #blacklivesmatter may prompt some of your friends to question whether or not you believe #alllivesmatter. If you post about the death penalty, you may be questioned about your concern for unborn babies. Your best intentions are often met with accusations that you don't care about enough things or the correct things. You will be misunderstood or questioned. You may even be un-friended or blocked. As you face questions, you may consider staying silent.

I appreciate my friend Tina's response when she's ques-tioned about her beliefs: "I'm always questioned as to how I can have leather shoes and be a vegetarian. I say I do my best." Tina's response models a humility and willingness to acknowledge her limitations. She isn't defensive. She's honest. We are all doing our best with what we know and are able to do. That posture reminds me of a quote from Maya Angelou: "I did then what I knew how to do. Now that I know better, I do better."[1]

We were created to be in relationship with one another; we're embodied souls capable of communicating with one another in a multitude of ways. If we truly believe we are the body with each of us as a different part but connected and dependent on one another, our failure isn't ours to bear alone. We are one body. We are bound to be misunderstood. We are bound to make mistakes. We are bound to learn. We are bound together. Someone else's win is our win.

We learn by trying. I've tried to be a runner . . . I'm not a runner. I've never experienced the so-called runner's high, and despite the science behind endorphin production, I'm convinced the runner's high is something runners make up to fool others into joining their folly. The only thing I find stranger than running is paying to run, but that's exactly what motivates my husband and daughter. They register for races, pay good money, train like they mean it, and then run the races. Did I mention they pay money to do this?

My part in this process, other than to complain about the long training runs that happen on precious weekends as well as to complain about their complaining about the long runs, is to be their nutritionist, trainer, and cheerleader. I don't want to run or cross the finish line, but I want to be at the finish line to cheer on my runners with cowbells, signs, and diaphragm-supported screaming. Sometimes I will run a few miles with Peter or Bethany if they need someone to fall behind and make them feel like they are keeping a good pace.

I will make sure we have eggs and chicken for lean sources of protein, and I make sure they stay hydrated and stretch. I've learned my part as a great cheerleader.

In other circumstances, the roles are reversed. Peter would rather train for a marathon or talk about beautiful margins on a dental crown for a patient than speak in front of an audience, but I would rather prep to speak in front of an audience every month than choose to run for hours at a time or floss my teeth. Perhaps that will change as I head deeper into my midlife crisis (I'm referring to running, though flossing daily will help as I age), but in the meantime, I know my part. I love to write and speak. He loves his work as a dentist, and he loves to run.

Now that you know I don't enjoy running, I'll let you in on another secret. I'm the least athletic person in the family. Elias participates in track and field events such as shot put and discus. Corban is a distance runner and decided he would try gymnastics for the first time when he was seventeen. Bethany is a dancer, and then there is my husband the runner. It has taken each of them years to figure out their "thing," and there were mistakes, failures, and a few moments of perfection in those journeys.

Watching their journeys taught me as much about each individual finding their part, their race, and their voice as it has about envy and jealousy. Envy is a desire to have something someone else has. Jealousy is a resentment stemming from wrongfully believing someone else has something you deserve. I envy my children's energy and resilience; each one of them has tried their hand at distance running, and all three have placed dead last more than once. In my most honest moments when I'm in an unhealthy space, I will not try anything if there is a chance I will fail. Even writing this book took checking my own broken heart as I looked longingly at the commercial success and growing platform of others first with envy and then with jealousy.

FINDING YOUR VOICE ISN'T A COMPETITION

It's rather easy to compare ourselves to others in a self-imposed competition. Mary, the mother of Jesus, and her cousin Elizabeth could've served as the perfect example of a catfight ripe for a bad movie script—two pregnant women, each carrying a child destined for greatness. However, theirs is a story of mutual respect and honoring. Their friendship reminds us that sometimes we need to seek the presence and help of others along our journey of finding our voice.

Mary, upon hearing from an angel the disconcerting news that she was pregnant with the Son of God and that her aging cousin Elizabeth also was with child, has a short response that's to the point: "I am the servant of the Lord; let it be to me according to your word" (Luke 1:38, ESV). And then Mary travels to be with Elizabeth. No one would blame Mary had she stayed silent in shock or out of fear. It makes sense culturally for the younger Mary to find comfort and safety in the elder Elizabeth's presence. The visit could've been Mary's solo babymoon. And it could've been awkward, but instead there is no second thought as to whose child will be more powerful than the other's.

Elizabeth is unafraid and generous in her word of blessing and exhortation. I imagine that's because she knows what I often have to remind myself: finding and using our voice isn't a zero-sum game where we compete with others. Elizabeth isn't competing. She knows this is a journey for both of them, and she sets the stage for Mary to speak out words we now call the Magnificat. Elizabeth isn't there just to provide an audience or to be a foil or competitor. She's the one whose presence and words remind Mary who she is and what is to come.

Encourage others to find their voice as you find yours. Part of learning to speak up is also about encouraging others to do the same. Our personal growth and development doesn't happen in a vacuum. We were created with community and mutual flourishing in mind. That is why it's important to help others even as we are trying to figure out our own voice.

VERBAL OR WRITTEN ENCOURAGEMENT

I have been married for twenty-five years, and I still don't know how to read my husband's mind. Peter hasn't mastered the art either. We actually need to communicate with words—spoken and written. Years ago, our marriage therapist told us to overcommunicate because people who have been in a long-term relationship mistakenly begin to assume too many things in regards to intentions or desire. I know many of my blog readers (my Dear Readers) and friends cheered for me as I took on this book project, but I can't express how much it has meant to me to have a small group of friends encourage me, check up on my progress, and remind me that my writing is about faithfulness, not about achieving success or comparing my work to others.

Don't underestimate the power behind words of encouragement. If you are able to recognize someone else's voice in their writing, art, or other endeavors, let them know it. I didn't think I was good at writing and public speaking until teachers such as Elizabeth Johnson, Karen Umlauf, Stuart Ciske, and Larry Studt encouraged me with feedback, critique, and affirmation. When my son Corban was a senior in high school, he joined the academic decathlon team at the behest of his teacher and cross country coach, Mark. Corban, ever the play-it-cool child, took second place in literature with no previous academic decathlon experience. I wrote an email to thank Coach Mark for seeing something in him that no other teachers had named—potential.

If you have the time and want to make the time, sit down and write a handwritten note. I enjoy the ease and immediacy of texting, but there's also a beauty to slowing down, handwriting a note, and sending it off the old-fashioned way. After the November 2016 elections, many movements asked people to handwrite postcards to politicians because they understood the power of written words sent by individual people collectively communicating a message.

As Christians, we should also remember to turn to the Bible every day to be encouraged and challenged in Scripture. The Bible is God's word of encouragement to us to be faithful to the gifts we have been given so that God's kingdom comes on earth as it is in heaven. Words are not empty.

PRAYER

My children don't have the kind of grandparent/grandchild relationship usually depicted in pop culture. There is no doubt that there is mutual love and respect, but there still remains a wide cultural gap between my immigrant parents and their American-born grandchildren, of which four are biracial. My parents look at their grandchildren and see the fruit not only of their sacrifices but also of their prayers.

If you don't know any Korean immigrant Christians, you're missing out. Praying is one of their love languages. Prayer is not an afterthought or used to mark the beginning of a meal or the end the day. For my parents' generation, prayer is the way they start their day. I know my parents pray every morning, probably before any of us are even awake, for their two daughters, two sons-in-law, and seven grandchildren. It's fitting that their language of love would be prayer because it transcends what we cannot between my limited Korean and their limited English (their English is better than my Korean).

It's also only in prayer that any of us can put our own agendas aside—for one another and for ourselves—because we are in a posture of humility. When Bethany announced her request to pursue dance, Peter and I knew we couldn't respond without praying. Anything that was going to come out of my mouth at that moment would be about me, not about Bethany—who God had created her to be and become in her maturity and development. Prayer helped us remember that this was her journey and we all had roles to play. Prayer isn't a quick stop to a vending machine. It's about acknowledging our humanity and God's sovereignty.

SHOW UP

The gift of presence is another one of those things I had to learn to understand and appreciate. My parents weren't the white American parents or the non-Korean parents I saw on television or that my friends talked about. We didn't really do things together or talk about life. They were busy working, and when they weren't working, they were recovering from working and surviving in a culture new to them. There was no time and limited communication—due to our language differences—for us to talk in the manner Peter and I do with our children. However, I've come to understand that they have always been and continue to be present for and available to us.

I have a photograph of my parents and in-laws sitting at our kitchen table shortly after Bethany was born. No one is talking, and because this was 1995, no one was staring at the not-yet-developed smartphone. All four grandparents are clearly sitting in silence, staring in the direction of the fruit plate set before them. I used to look at the photograph and think about the awkwardness and distance I thought I saw in the photo. But now I understand that all four of them were offering their gift of presence to the parents of a newborn. They continued to show up.

Sometimes we will need someone to show up and push us to speak up. I want to be that kind of mentor, and as I'm an older Korean American woman, it's culturally easier and appropriate for me to assume the role of "auntie." Esther had Mordecai—who showed up at the gate wearing ashes and sackcloth. Moses had Aaron—and Moses knew that even though he was the leader, he was a better leader with his brother at his side. And David had Nathan—the king and a prophet.

SPEAKING TRUTH TO POWER

There isn't a lot of background to explain King David's working relationship with Nathan. David was the king, and Nathan was the prophet. For this type of relationship to work there had to be a level of mutual respect even though power remained unequal.

The king didn't have to take orders or suggestions from the prophet, but sometimes a stamp of approval was nice. In 2 Samuel 7, both men initially believed David's idea to build a temple to protect the Ark of the Covenant was a worthy one. But during the night, Nathan received a word from God challenging their notions of who was to build the temple (answer: not David), who would initiate the building of a temple (answer: not David), and what was in store for David (answer: a line of succession that never ends). Nathan could've chosen to keep the interaction with God to himself but instead faithfully and courageously confronts his king and suggests this isn't the time to build. Sometimes, speaking up to power means telling someone your advice was wrong, and it's time to reconsider a decision.

Next, Nathan has to confront David's domino-chain of sin involving Uriah and Bathsheba, which starts when King David is fighting off insomnia by taking a stroll on his roof. He spots a beautiful woman who happens to be bathing. David snoops around to find out her identity and learns she is Bathsheba, wife to Uriah, who happens to be on the battlefield as a loyal member of the king's army. David doesn't see this as problem at all and orders his men to bring Bathsheba to him and rapes her. At this point, no one stands up to David to tell him this is a horrible idea, and Bathsheba has no rights or armed guards to protect her. She gets pregnant, and it's the king's child.

Instead of owning up to the situation, King David digs his hole of sin and shame deeper by ordering Uriah off the battlefield in hopes that Uriah, on this unexpected leave from war, will go home and have sex with his wife. Uriah is a man of honor and chooses to stay with the king's servants just outside of the palace. King David is so desperate to cover up his tracks that he invites Uriah to dinner and gets him drunk, hoping that he might wander back home. No, Uriah stays put.

So King David, at his wit's end, sets up a military situation where Uriah is sent to the worst part of the battle and then left alone with no reinforcements. David essentially sends Uriah out to battle alone to die. His orders are given to and executed by Joab, Uriah's commander. Does Joab speak up and tell his king this is a horrible idea? No, and Uriah dies on the battlefield. Once Uriah is dead, David is free to bring Bathsheba into his house, add her to his family, and legitimize their son.

This is a picture of how power unchecked against even the most vulnerable and faithful is so obviously wrong, and how that same unchecked power blinds the powerful to see their complicity in the sin of injustice. God sends Nathan to confront the king. Nathan speaks up, despite the fact that the king could reject the accusation, ignore the call to repentance, and order Nathan's death. In 2 Samuel 12, Nathan uses a beautiful parable to get David to drop his guard, to stop operating out of self-preservation mode, and to see that it's obviously wrong to take advantage of people and violently take what isn't his. Nathan doesn't shy away from a potentially deadly confrontation with David but carefully waits for David to reflect, recognize, and repent.

What are the situations and circumstances where some courage and creative storytelling can help you speak truth to power just like Nathan did with David? Is there a situation at work involving a boss or more senior member of your team? Is there a toxic relational dynamic in your life that needs to be addressed? Learn from and take to heart the story of how Nathan handled this situation. He didn't accuse David but painted a picture of empathy and connection to draw out an opportunity for change. When we remember King David as a great leader, we can't forget that he became a great leader because of Nathan.

FINANCIAL SUPPORT

When it comes to encouraging others to find their voice, we might want to consider putting our money where other's mouths and voices are. We can financially support artists, spaces, and retreats for people who steward their gifts well. We can support talented individuals and organizations that are doing the work about the issues we care most about.

Peter, Bethany, and I were blown away by the quick and generous response to a Facebook post I wrote on February 28, 2017:

"Bigly request. Anyone out there with extra airline miles or money to burn? Bethany Chang just got an invitation to audition in NYC during her break here at home."

I'm not sure if I really believed something would come of the post, but I put it out there. I went to bed trying to decide which credit card to use for the airline ticket. The next morning, I saw that two friends had shared the post with their networks. Within two days, we had two friends, Lincoln L. and Anthony K., offer to help an aspiring artist head back to NYC for an audition. (Bethany was offered an apprenticeship with the dance company.)

Do you know of an artist who could use a new paintbrush or canvas? Do you know of a writer who would appreciate a gift card for coffee at her favorite writing spot in a coffee shop or a weekend in a cabin to work on a project? Do you know of a community volunteer who would benefit from a massage or even a movie ticket for a night off? Do you know of an aspiring recording artist who is launching a social fundraising campaign? If you can't give money, do you know people who could provide professional or technical support?

Let's take it a step further. Think of the people who are the prophets of your community. They are the ones who willingly pay the cost and take the risks to speak out, and they certainly don't do it for monetary gain. They are in our Twitter and Facebook feeds. We can read what they write because there are no paywalls on their blogs. We learn from them in the public square and consume their work. How can we, as their community, leverage our finances to make sure they are also rested and rewarded? Let me give two suggestions.

First, if you have any influence in how a church or organization pays guest speakers, please make sure all guest speakers are paid equitably. If you are a person with that kind of influence, you know the ins and outs of church budgets, and you might even be aware of speaker rates and agent fees. You know if and when women or people of color are paid less than the big name. Do what you can to make sure that nonsense stops.

And second, if you are a consumer of books and conferences, be a savvier consumer. If racial, ethnic, and gender diversity is important to you, then you should pay attention to who publishers are publishing and who is on stage as a speaker or panelist. Give feedback when values and representation that matter to you aren't reflected on the platforms addressing the issues you care about. The Christian industrial complex is actually a thing. Conferencing, agents, sponsorships, endorsements, influencer perks, branding—these are not limited to the secular corporate world. This is all part of Christian business where certain speakers and authors, who most often are white, have developed a personal brand. And don't think for a moment that this isn't also a business because it's called Christian. Aspiring and established authors may have literary agents. There are speaker agents and agencies with deep connections to churches, conferences, and other networked people in the industry. And just like in the music industry, Christian authors and speakers can cross over into nonreligious spaces.

I'm only a little judgmental. I certainly realize that I'm in and a part of this business. Mostly I'm concerned and confused as to how these powerful and influential spaces are dominated by white Christians—publishing, conferences, churches and denominational leadership, parachurch ministries, mission organizations, and on and on and on. I understand that, in order to stay in business, conference planners and publishers will sign authors and speakers who can sell tickets and books. So we need to use our voices and wallets to support organizations, publishers, and conferences we believe in—those that model kingdom values and a diverse picture of the kingdom. We need to encourage those in leadership to keep at it.

WAYS TO SPEAK UP

Fortunately for us, there are many ways in which we can use our voice. You *can* blog, tweet, or preach, but you don't *have* to blog, tweet, or preach in order to speak up.

Embodiment

When I think of the embodiment of using your body to speak out, I think of the Hebrew midwives Shiphrah and Puah. After the Pharaoh ordered all Hebrew baby boys to be killed at birth, they defied those orders because they "feared God and did not do what the king of Egypt had told them to do; they let the boys live" (Exodus 1:17). Think about it. Two Hebrew women, who could easily have said they had no power or voice, used their vocation as doulas and literally used their hands to actively protest and defy power. Then they straight up lied to the person in power despite the fact that their blatant civil disobedience was illegal. This wasn't risking a bad performance review. They risked death. They didn't pay lip service to the idea of raising their voice. They put their female bodies on the line to make sure baby boys survived the slaughter. They became the first example of civil disobedience in the face of a genocide initiated by an increasingly evil empire.

We see women and men embodying protest whether it's someone marching, or holding up a sign at a rally, or being attacked with water hoses while seeking to stop oil pipelines from crossing into sacred Native lands. We see social workers, whose physical presence reminds us there is hope in broken systems, and military chaplains, whose presence reminds soldiers there is still a place for hope and faith even in times of war.

Words and appearance

We also literally speak out. Words in casual conversation or prepared speeches are one of two primary ways I speak out. Whatever comes out of my mouth will always be connected to my physical presence as a Korean American cisgender woman. My wedding ring signals that I'm married. Sometimes I intentionally wear certain articles of clothing to further communicate and connect with my spoken words. Last year I had the opportunity to speak to Asian American ministry colleagues, and I knew what I would wear before I knew exactly what words I would speak. I wore an emerald green silk sheath dress and matching jacket my mother had custom made from fabric given to her by her mother-in-law. The outfit was one of several party dresses she had made in 1969 in anticipation of her new life in the United States. The dress was a symbol of dreams and hopes that did not materialize for my mother and, in some cases, skipped her and me. I knew the dress connected me physically to the words I would eventually use to speak about faithfully ministering without necessarily experiencing personally the end result.

Dress

Another way to wear your heart and voice on your sleeve is to dress a certain way. Back in the day, politicians produced campaign buttons supporters could wear. That has given way to the message T-shirt as another way to embody voice.

Dr. Chanequa Walker-Barnes, an author, professor, and activist, has said her travel uniform is a comfortable pair of jeans, sneakers, and a message T-shirt, knowing full well that reactions to her message T-shirts often fall between racial lines.[2] Her fashion sensibilities have inspired me also to wear my voice. As I was packing for a work trip to a southern state, Corban joked about my penchant for wearing message T-shirts for travel—but then he changed his tone. He asked me not to wear a specific T-shirt because he was concerned people would respond to the message not with warmth or approval but rather with disagreement that could lead to a verbal exchange or physical altercation. Corban and I both understand the power of words worn on the body of an Asian American woman.

Space

Another way many people of color embody their voice is by occupying and being physically present in predominantly white spaces. For some of us that includes our neighborhoods, workplaces, and even churches. Sometimes our mere presence in a space disrupts business as usual.

Disembodied words, symbols, and images

We can also speak up by using our words separate from our physical bodies. This is where social media posts, blogs, and letters to your government representatives come into play. We can speak up by putting our words out into the virtual cloud or physical mailbox and perhaps never know what impact our words have on others, which is why I chose to describe this as *disembodied* words. Writing is the other way I speak up, and my hope is that when readers who have only engaged with my written words finally hear me speak or meet me in person, they "hear" the same person.

The power to impact is limited by technology and the size of our personal networks, which are broader than ever due to technology. While the boom years of mommy bloggers has perhaps peaked, there is still a growing space to speak out in the virtual world with the articles we post, the questions we ask, and the answers we exchange in our virtual communities. But remember, speaking up is never a question of gaining audience size. It's an act of obedience and faithfulness.

There has been a steady resurgence of hand lettering or calligraphy. Even as digital graphic art continues to develop, many people have returned to the practice of picking up a pen and speaking up by using beautiful, patient, intentional strokes of ink. This isn't a fluke. As technology continues to develop, there will be a pull of nostalgia and desire to connect with one another in old-fashioned ways. There will always be power in the written word to speak up. Calligraphy artist Ellie Yang Camp says putting words to paper requires a settling down in her own body and breathing to steady her hand, which helps her focus.[3] This reminds us that speaking up isn't about only the audience but is also about the impact on our lives.

I would be remiss to not include two unique types of digital graphic art—the meme and the gif. A meme combines words and an image to communicate something as concrete as a one-word declaration like "Yesssss!" Sometimes they use an image of a cat appearing to raise its paw in the air, and sometimes it's something more ethereal such as a line of poetry combined with the image of a beautiful sunset as the background. A gif, which is a short video on a loop (with or without words), is also meant to communicate a brief declaration or something more emotionally ambiguous like a sarcastic "Yay!"

Several years ago, I asked my husband, who served as a captain in the US Air Force, if he would like to have an American flag to fly on certain holidays. I'm not particularly patriotic, but I also realized that Peter has a different relationship than me to the symbols of our country. Our flag is out July 4 and Memorial Day—up in the morning and down with the sun, according to the guidelines. Sometimes it hangs upside down as a way to communicate to our neighbors how we and communities of color are experiencing distress in our country. The "No Solicitors" sticker on our front door rarely seems to work, but signs and stickers on homes or vehicles also have been a way for people to claim their voice.

Art

Thankfully there are some people in the world who speak up through the art they create. Graffiti and street art has always been a way for people to physically leave their mark. The British artist Banksy, for example, highlighted graffiti as public art and public protest.[4] Artist and sculptor Michael Murphy used toy plastic guns suspended in mid-air to create an optical illusion where the guns formed a map of the United States when viewed from one angle and a large rifle when viewed from another. The installation titled "Identity Crisis" was created in response to the ever-present but unresolved debate on gun ownership in order to elicit more conversation.[5]

Other artists such as David Young Kim[6] integrate faith, activism, and cultural roots[7] into commercial murals and exhibition works. In 2015, Kim created art installations for the students attending the Evangelical Covenant Church's triennial youth CHIC conference. One interactive art installation used Post-its; another exhibit was a large-scale stations of the cross created with twelve twenty-five-by-four-foot-long banners painted in black paint on white paper that hung from the convention room ceilings. Students walked past each station, their gaze forced up beyond what is normally comfortable.

Raising Her Voice

Maggie Hubbard is a painter based in the Chicago suburbs (see her website at www.maggiehubbard.net). I met Maggie at a youth conference where she created a painting while a speaker was presenting on stage. She did this twice a day for four days. Since that time, I've noticed a shift in what she's communicating in her work.[a]

Question: So tell me about the shift in your work and your use of social media.

Answer: When we met, my artwork was based in personal and familial loss as my father had recently died. But that conference and time of life was a catalyst for the work I am currently doing. The combination of connecting with Christians doing social justice work, paying attention to the Black Lives Matter movement, and connecting more with the LGBTQIA community as my brother came out—I would say those three things shifted my work as a painter and individual. I moved out to Seattle, attended a multiethnic church, and started deconstructing my faith, traditions, and assumptions.

The paintings I made (and continue to make) within this shift are depicting what I'm learning and deconstructing. As an artist, it is rather intimidating to share the work that speaks to my personal growth process, but I think it's important to share. The idea isn't to display my life but rather to create possible connections between people and a piece of art that is questioning problematic aspects of our society. Art has the ability to transform seemingly normal things into so much more.

I can draw strong connections between my previous work in grieving the loss of my father to the more sociopolitical work I am doing now. It's almost as if I have established a practice of visually grieving. Grieving inequities, racial divides, ignorance, power, privilege, whiteness. . . . My father's death taught me a lot about needing to accept reality even when that reality is extremely hard to hold. So practicing lament through my art has allowed me to look at society and begin to sort out what is good, what is difficult, what is harmful.

Social media allows me to immediately share this in public view, and that's a little weird. It feels quite vulnerable [but] it's all [my choice]. . . . No one is asking me to post the work that I am doing.

Q: Were you hesitant to share your newer work?

A: There were definitely times I was apprehensive of sharing—fear of ruffling feathers, fear of having to speak to something I'm not ready to speak to, not wanting to come across as a fully knowledgeable person.

Q: What's your advice to people who are reluctant to speak up?

A: Listen to people. I know, for myself, it feels uncomfortable to highlight issues; I would much rather diffuse a situation than actually speak up about it. . . . But I have friends who hold me to looking at things critically and friends affirming the work I am doing. There have been intimidating steps along the way, but I look back and see how my core group of friends has influenced my artwork through their own vocations, questions, and ideas.

Also, having in-person dialogue with people who I imagine would disagree with me has been helpful. I can develop a lot of fear in my mind that actually isn't grounded in real experience. When I have hard-nosed white individuals saying to me, "Your work is good, it's making me ask questions," the internal fear lessens. Again and again it shows me that, as a white woman, there is not much danger in speaking up.

I would say there is a genuine social risk. I'm curious how social media may end the conversation rather than start it, but social media allows for a much wider conversation to happen. I want to continue this work in love. I genuinely believe whiteness and white thinking is harmful to our society, to both people of color and white people. So people keep me focused . . . [and give me] a desire to see wholeness in the communities I am a part of.

[a]*Personal interview with the author, October 18, 2017.*

Textile artists who speak through their knitted and crocheted works of art spread their message when people wear their creations through different seasons of weather and life. Embroidery, seemingly a dead art in recent generations, has also seen a comeback. People are using an old skill—which some might argue was sexist because it was only taught to women—as a means of communicating new slogans and sayings with the staying power of thread and fabric. Some

knitters and crochet aficionados have taken their skills to the
streets in an art form known as yarn bombing, covering
random, everyday things such as bike racks, door handles,
sign posts, and even trees in colorful patterns in a way that
draws attention and creates beauty in some unlikely spaces.

Spoken word artists connect words in rhythm and rhyme
and draw us deeper into stories that matter not just to us
personally but also to us all. Musicians and lyricists capture
time and space into melodies and choruses that we may
remember into our dying days. Performers such as Beyoncé
capture their own journeys and metamorphoses. In response
to Beyoncé's groundbreaking album "Lemonade," other voices
expanded on that original work through critiques, lectures,
and additional resources that engaged in the cultural, spiritual,
and political impact of its messages. One of the most prominent examples of this amplification is Candice Benbow's
"Lemonade Syllabus." Benbow, a doctoral student in religion
and society at Princeton Theological Seminary and a lecturer
in women's and gender studies at Rutgers University, pulled
together a treasure trove of resources and recommended
readings based on the themes of "Lemonade," recognizing
that the album and videos were not just entertainment to be
consumed but also were commentaries and responses to
current events.[8]

Dancers connect movement to sound or silence in varying
levels of light and distraction, reminding us that our bodies
speak out in ways that are universal as well as unique to cultures and history. For example, innovator Homer Bryant of
the Chicago Multicultural Dance Center developed and teaches

"Hiplet" (a combination of hip hop and ballet) to make dance more accessible to low-income and black students by addressing implicit bias and racism in the classical ballet world.[9]

There are still moments when I listen to music (I learned to play and eventually quit the piano, flute, piccolo, and guitar), look at a piece of modern art (those canvases painted entirely in one color), or watch my daughter dance (did I mention I was in a Korean folk dancing troupe?), and I recognize in myself a hint of envy and a touch of jealousy wishing for the mastery of another artistic skill, but words—spoken and written—are my voice.

Not everyone can hear the message of hope or faith through a song, see it in a piece of art, or feel it as they watch a dancer move. Sometimes people need to read or hear the words spoken by a person. Some respond to the messages of visual artists, musicians, and dancers; others respond to the neighbors who offer up conversation, opinions, and challenges to the status quo. We can't all be the hands or the feet or the eyes of the body—we all certainly need each other. And we all need time and practice to find our unique voice and learn to use it. As my wise friend and fellow road-tripper Tina commented, "We need a diversity of viewpoints, of people, and of delivery."

Our God is the Creator who gave us many ways to hear, see, smell, taste, and feel. There are many ways to raise our voices for faith, hope, and love. May we all be faithful, and may we all honor and lift up one another's histories, skills, and opportunities to speak up for faith, hope, and love. We were not meant to be silent.

*M*y daughter was the only one in her high school graduating class who had her own hashtag: #flymysweet.

Initially, she thought it was weird, and she took every opportunity to let me know. But as the months went on, she came to understand it was my way of coping with the transition we were making, inviting others into our journey, and communicating my love and blessing. My sons also thought the hashtag was weird but soon asked when they would receive theirs. Senior year in high school is when each child receives their unique twenty-first century blessing. Corban's was #runmyson.

My first draft of this book was finished one month out from Bethany's college graduation. When she had previously announced that she was on track to graduate early, Peter and I had spent some time trying to talk her out of it. The possibility of reducing her student loans and our parent loans by a year was a great incentive, but we were concerned about her jumping too quickly into the "real world." Late nights with bad dorm food and friendships forged over hectic schedules of rehearsals and exams are a unique time that can't be repeated in grad school or in an apartment with friends. All three of our children can repeat my words of advice as they each headed into high school: "The goal is not to peak in high school. High school is the springboard to life beyond the bubble. Dad and I were both late bloomers, and see how great things turned out for us!"

But we were now way past high school with Bethany. Graduating from college early would mean cutting short a time of life that can't be repeated—adulthood suspended in a bigger bubble with fewer responsibilities.

Bethany wasn't fazed by it. She wanted to dive deeply and swiftly into her dreams of dancing and choreographing, and she was unwavering in her determination. During my first draft of this book, she considered her options, looked for more auditions, and took classes in Chicago and New York. During the time of the first round of rewrites for this book, we were packing and then unpacking the minivan, moving her into her first apartment. She had secured two paid part-time gigs that would cover her budget and give her the flexibility to audition and take dance classes. She had culled her suburban wardrobe to one more compatible with the city that would fit into her city bedroom. She edited her personal belongings of memorabilia, kitsch, and artwork she had begun collecting. She even cut her own hair into a youthful-but-edgy bob, saving money and showing the world she was experimenting with how and what she would project of herself. Bethany is testing out her voice, and it's both exhilarating and frightening to watch from this side.

Ultimately, I want to protect her from failure, from falling flat on her face—but I know this is her part of the journey. I know how painful, humiliating, and lonely falling and failing can be. If there were a way to protect her, I would. People see so many similarities between the two of us, and we can recognize more as we both grow even more comfortable in our skin and with our unique voices. But I've also seen the differences between the two of us. For example, take the protest signs we made for the Women's March on Washington:

Set number one:

"If it is not intersectional it is not feminism."
"Take your broken heart and make it into art."
"If you cut off my reproductive choice can I cut off yours?"

Set number two:

"#yellowperil for #blacklivesmatter"
"Remember that consciousness is power.
—Yuri Kochiyama"
"We are all part of one another. —Yuri Kochiyama"

Can you hear it? See it? The signs are similar but different. Her voice is different. I can't wait to keep hearing and seeing what she has to say. Will she resonate with Esther or Moses? Will she use her vocation and body like Shiphrah and Puah, or speak truth to power like Nathan?

And I'm wondering what you will do. I realize we have not journeyed together like I have with my daughter. To many of you, I'm a new voice that you've been reading or hearing for the first time. Others of you know my voice and are waiting for the familiar greeting. So here goes.

My Dear Readers,

After some forty thousand words together, let me welcome the first-timers into the fold. I hope you have learned a little more about your voice and how God might be inviting you to use it today.

Even though Bethany has left her childhood bedroom, I still have a front-row seat to her journey. We text, Facetime, Snapchat, use FindMyFriends to literally find each other, and stalk each other on Instagram. I get to see and hear how she raises her voice.

I wish I could have a front-row seat to your journey, or at least a backstage pass. I wish there was a way to sit down with you and have a glass of something-something and talk about what you connected with, what questions you have, what you are learning, what you disagree with, and what you are trying. I'm not sure I want to know *exactly* what you're thinking now that you've finished the book. It feels very vulnerable to ask you to respond to this book, which is me putting my voice into action, but feedback is also part of the process. Find me on social media, and let's sharpen one another. Deal?

God is inviting you into a deeper understanding of who you are in the context of your family, community, workplace, and church. May you test out your voice, make some mistakes, work through the reasons you stay silent, and find courage to speak up. This world desperately needs the good news, and it will need diverse voices from different perspectives. I can't wait to hear and see what's next for you!

ACKNOWLEDGMENTS

WHERE I FORGET SOMEONE BUT STILL TRY

*P*eter, thank you for always trying to do right by me, for laughing with me, for staying in your lane by buying me wine and not buying me coffee, and for loving, respecting, and honoring me as your equal.

Bethany, you are my favorite. I miss hearing your voice and watching you dance in the aisles of all of our favorite stores. Thank you for teaching me how to live fully in the moment and to not take myself so seriously. And, yes, I will take whatever fitness class you want even if it means I fall on my face like I did with that crazy machine thingy.

Corban, you are my favorite. I miss eating lunch with you and watching you love your friends with integrity and loyalty. Thank you for teaching me to set goals and take big risks. This summer you are going to help me land a handstand.

Elias, you are my favorite. I am trying to take in the remaining time we have together before you head off to college, listening to you laugh and riff on the bass. Thank you for teaching me to be joyful and spontaneous. Let's go to Menchie's for dinner!

Mom and Dad, Umma and Abbah, thank you for forcing me to learn Korean and keep a journal. Thank you for all the sacrifices you continue to make, and for your prayers of protection and blessing. The Napa Ladies—Bora, Christie, Grace, Jinhee, Nikki, Priscilla, Sabrina, and Tracey; the Supper Club Ladies—Jennifer, Marissa, Monique, Patti, Tina, and honorary member Melissa; and the Voxer/Texting Ladies—Amena, Deidra, Janna, Jennifer, Jo, Nish, Sandra, and Vickie; thank you all for being a part of my life. I wish you could all meet in real life; I think the universe would explode. You have been my sounding board, my cheerleaders, and my reality check. In a world where raising your voice can easily make neighbors into enemies, you all have remained loyal friends who keep me humble and grounded.

Thanks to IVP and specifically Cindy Bunch, who made eye contact with me whenever she had the chance and asked me if I had any book ideas; Helen Lee, who continues to encourage me to blaze trails while she blazes trails as well; and my editor, Al Hsu, whose belief in "project snowball" more than a decade ago helped me find my writing voice.

And, of course, thanks be to God who invites all of us to be fully present and fully whole in mind, body, and spirit.

DISCUSSION QUESTIONS

CHAPTER 1: SEEN BUT NOT HEARD

1. What happens to the church and its witness when people are silenced?
2. How does the good news get communicated if only white men are heard and encouraged to speak out?
3. How have you felt silenced or silenced others?
4. What gives you the courage to speak up?

CHAPTER 2: WHO AM I?

1. What parts of your personal story have you avoided?
2. How have you tried to hide those stories from others?
3. What are you afraid those stories say about you?
4. Go back through some of the more difficult parts of your story and look for how God is working for good. How does looking through God's work in your story change the way you see yourself and God?

CHAPTER 3: LEARNING TO SPEAK

1. If you could make a positive impact on one issue involving your family, community, or the world, what would you tackle?

2. When you watch or read the news, what are the things that make you talk back to the television or mutter under your breath? What do you say?

3. How could you take those words and raise your voice about what you deeply care about?

CHAPTER 4: FEAR AND FAILURE

1. What keeps you from speaking up when you know something needs to be said?

2. What is something you wish you had said or done but chose to stay silent or do nothing?

3. How would you handle that situation differently and why?

4. When you think about something you want to speak up about, what are you most afraid will happen if you raise your voice?

5. How does fear and failure factor into the way you make other decisions in your life?

CHAPTER 5: IRL (IN REAL LIFE)

1. How do you choose to communicate your values and opinions and ask questions in an honest way with the people you consistently interact with in real life?

2. How does that change the way you feel about using your voice or how you use your voice?

3. What keeps you from speaking up in social settings?

4. Where is home for you, and how do you describe being at home?

5. What is it like for you to be at home with the people you feel most at home with?

6. What people are the most difficult to be honest with?

7. What makes speaking up with those people difficult?

CHAPTER 6: WHEN YOU POST IT

1. How can communicating in the digital world be used to create and steward creation?

2. How can your values as a Christ-follower be reflected in the comments you make, the posts you share, and the images you promote?

3. How can you use social media to speak up and speak out?

CHAPTER 7: EVERYONE HAS A PART

1. What do you think is the difference between unity and conformity?

2. How does that influence the way you live out your faith through your skills and gifts?

3. What are your unique ways of speaking out, and how can you grow in developing your voice?

4. As you develop your own voice and speak up, how can you encourage others to do the same?

NOTES

1 Seen but Not Heard

[1]"Word Root of Vocation," *Merriam-Webster Dictionary*, www.merriam -webster.com/dictionary/vocation.

[2]Carl Richards, "Learning to Deal with the Impostor Syndrome," *New York Times*, www.nytimes.com/2015/10/26/your-money/learning-to-deal-with -the-impostor-syndrome.html?mcubz=0.

[3]Joe Langford and Pauline Rose Clance, "The Impostor Phenomenon: Recent Research Findings Regrading Dynamics, Personality and Family Patterns and Their Implications for Treatment," *Psychotherapy* 30, no. 3 (Fall 1993), www.paulineroseclance.com/pdf/-Langford.pdf.

[4]"Barefoot, Status," *Dictionary of Biblical Imagery*, ed. Leland Ryken, James C. Wilhoit, and Tremper Longman III (Downers Grove, IL: IVP Academic, 1998), 74.

[5]"Sandal," *Dictionary of Bible Themes*, Bible Gateway, www.biblegateway .com/resources/dictionary-of-bible-themes/5179-sandal.

3 Learning to Speak

[1]Saul McLeod, "Jean Piaget," *Simply Psychology* (2015), www.simplypsy chology.org/piaget.html.

[2]My paraphrase and summary of the work of James W. Fowler, *Stages of Faith* (New York: HarperCollins, 1981), 117-99.

[3]Daniel Hill, *White Awake* (Downers Grove, IL: InterVarsity Press, 2017), 4.

[4]For more on The Crane Project, see www.thecraneproject.org.

[5]For more about Communities First Association, see https://cfapartners.org.

[6]Deray McKesson, Twitter, https://twitter.com/deray/status/852356723 100831744.

[7]This content first appeared on my blog, Kathy Khang, "Saunas and Sheet Masks: A Theology of Self-Care," kathykhang.com, February 1, 2017, www .kathykhang.com/2017/02/01/saunas-sheet-masks-theology-self-care.

[8]Audre Lorde, *A Burst of Light: And Other Essays* (Ithaca, NY: Firebrand Books, 1988), 130.

[9]Anna Almendrala, "More Than a Third of Americans Don't Get Enough Sleep," *HuffPost*, February 19, 2016, www.huffingtonpost.com/entry /americans-arent-getting-enough-sleep_us_56c61306e4b0b40245c9687b.

4 Fear and Failure

[1]Soong-Chan Rah, Evangelicals for Justice meeting, Chicago, July 28-29, 2017.

[2]To learn more about the actual first Thanksgiving, see Robert Tracy McKenzie, *The First Thanksgiving* (Downers Grove, IL: InterVarsity Press, 2013).

[3]Alex Altman, "Person of the Year: Black Lives Matter," *Time*, http://time .com/time-person-of-the-year-2015-runner-up-black-lives-matter.

[4]"'American Idol' runner-up Bo Bice says he was called 'white boy' at Popeyes," Fox News, January 4, 2017, www.foxnews.com/entertainment /2017/01/04/american-idol-runner-up-bo-bice-says-was-called-white-boy -at-popeyes.html.

[5]C. N. Le, "14 Important Statistics About Asian Americans," Asian Nation, November 29, 2017, www.asian-nation.org/14-statistics.shtml.

[6]Erika Lee, *The Making of Asian America* (New York: Simon & Schuster, 2015), 3.

5 IRL (In Real Life)

[1]Census Viewer, "Libertyville, Illinois Population: Census 2010 and 2000 Interactive Map, Demographics, Statistics, Quick Facts," http://census viewer.com/city/IL/Libertyville.

[2]For more on the term *white fragility*, see Robin DiAngelo, "White Fragility," *The International Journal of Critical Pedagogy* 3, no. 3 (2011).

6 WHEN YOU POST IT

[1]See Kathy Khang, "In Times of Dire Distress," kathykhang.com, December 4, 2014, www.kathykhang.com/2014/12/04/in-times-of-dire-distress.

[2]See Molly Soat, "Social Medial Triggers a Dopamine High," *Marketing News*, American Marketing Association, November 2015, www.ama.org/publications/MarketingNews/Pages/feeding-the-addiction.aspx.

[3]See Stuart Wolpert, "The Teenage Brain on Social Media," UCLA Newsroom, May 31, 2016, http://newsroom.ucla.edu/releases/the-teenage-brain-on-social-media.

[4]Soat, "Social Medial Triggers a Dopamine High."

[5]Gregory A. Smith and Jessica Martínez, "How the Faithful Voted: A Preliminary 2016 Analysis," Pew Research Center, November 9, 2016, www.pewresearch.org/fact-tank/2016/11/09/how-the-faithful-voted-a-preliminary-2016-analysis.

[6]See Heather Caliri, "Dream Your Wildest Dream: One Woman's Yes with Kathy Khang," April 6, 2014, www.heathercaliri.com/2014/04/06/owy-kathy-khang.

[7]See Be the Bridge to Racial Unity, Facebook, www.facebook.com/groups/BetheBridge.

[8]See Be the Bridge, https://beabridgebuilder.com/about.

7 EVERYONE HAS A PART

[1]Maya Angelou, Oprah's Life Class video, Oprah.com, October 19, 2011, www.oprah.com/oprahs-lifeclass/the-powerful-lesson-maya-angelou-taught-oprah-video.

[2]Personal correspondence with the author, January 2018.

[3]For more on the calligraphy of Ellie Yang Camp, see www.thecraneproject.org.

[4]See Will Ellsworth-Jones, "The Story Behind Banksy," *Smithsonian Magazine*, February 2013, www.smithsonianmag.com/arts-culture/the-story-behind-banksy-4310304.

[5]See "Identity Crisis," Michael Murphy, Perceptual Art, http://perceptualart.com.

[6]See Dave Young Kim, Facebook, www.facebook.com/daveyoungkim.

[7]See "Dave Young Kim: Living Out a Calling as a Muralist," Faith & Leadership, February 23, 2016, www.faithandleadership.com/dave-young-kim-living-out-calling-muralist.

[8]See Candice Marie Benbow, "Lemonade Syllabus," May 6, 2016, www
.candicebenbow.com/lemonadesyllabus.

[9]See Andrea Marks, "Why Are People So Riled Up About Black Girls Dancing
Hip-Hop on Pointe?," *Chicago Magazine*, June 9, 2016, www.chicagomag
.com/arts-culture/June-2016/Hip-Hop-Ballet-Hiplet-Homer-Bryant.

ABOUT THE AUTHOR

Kathy KyoungAh Khang is a writer, speaker, and yoga teacher. Her passion is partnering with other writers, speakers, creatives, pastors, and leaders to highlight and move the conversation forward on issues of race, ethnicity, and gender. She also has worked for more than twenty years for InterVarsity Christian Fellowship/USA and serves on the board of directors for both Evangelicals for Social Action and Sojourners. Kathy is a columnist for *Sojourners* magazine and is one of the authors of *More Than Serving Tea, DO BETTER Study Guide and Journal,* and *God's Graffiti Devotional.*

When Kathy's not staring at a computer screen, she enjoys life by reading, doing her nails, practicing yoga, or searching for the perfect pen and journal. She is married to Peter Chang, mom to three, and lives in the north suburbs of Chicago with no furry pets.

Connect with Kathy:

www.kathykhang.com

Twitter or Instagram: @mskathykhang

Facebook: kathykhangauthor

ALSO BY KATHY KHANG

Nikki A. Toyama and Tracey Gee, EDITORS
Kathy Khang, Christie Heller de Leon and Asifa Dean
CONSULTING EDITOR Jeanette Yep

More Than Serving Tea

ASIAN AMERICAN WOMEN ON
EXPECTATIONS, RELATIONSHIPS,
LEADERSHIP AND FAITH

"A distinctive anthology of Asian American voices speaking on issues of race,
gender, sexism and racism within the context of an overarching Christian faith."
CLAIRE S. CHOW
author of *Leaving Deep Water: The Lives of Asian-American Women at the Crossroads of Two Cultures*

More Than Serving Tea
978-0-8308-3371-9